Transcriptions • Lessons • Bios • Photos

25 GREAT COUNTRY GUITAR SOLOS

Featuring Legends of Lead Guitar, Including Chet Atkins, Brad Paisley, Vince Gill, Jerry Reed, Brent Mason, Pete Anderson, Merle Travis, Ray Flacke, Danny Gatton, and Many More

by Dave Rubin

T0081508

ALSO AVAILABLE:

25 Great Guitar Solos
HL00699721

25 Great Blues Guitar Solos
HL00699790

Chet Atkins, Merle Travis, and Jerry Reed cover photos provided by Michael Ochs Archives/Getty Images.

Pete Anderson cover photo © Michael Putland/Retna Ltd.

Vince Gill cover photo by Marc Morrison/Retna Ltd.

Brad Paisley cover photo © Beth Gwinn/Retna Ltd.

ISBN 978-1-4234-2640-0

HAL•LEONARD®
CORPORATION

7777 W. BLUEMOUND RD. P.O. BOX 13819 MILWAUKEE, WI 53213

Visit Hal Leonard Online at
www.halleonard.com

Preface

Country music has come a long way since Ernest Tubb's "Walking the Floor Over You," featuring Fay "Smitty" Smith (staff guitarist at Dallas radio station KGKO) on *electric* guitar, became a hit in 1941. At that time, amplified guitars were not allowed at the famed Grand Ole Opry, but Nashville's conservative powers that be recognized commercial potential when they heard it, and so lifted that antiquated ban in 1943. And when the Francis Craig Orchestra likewise passed that magic million mark with "Near You," in 1947, Nashville's modern era commenced.

The guitar has always the backbone of country music, even when it was used mainly to provide rhythm for fiddlers. But with the emergence in the late 1940s of Merle Travis and Chet Atkins—electric country guitar's foremost pioneers—the instrument was suddenly elevated to a new iconic status. In the early 1950s, pickers such as Jimmy Bryant, Joe Maphis, James Burton, and Hank Garland, all of who were blessed with amazing chops, far outpaced blues and many jazz musicians. And while that esteemed group was clean and fast, each successive generation of players, from Jerry Reed and Albert Lee to Jerry Donahue, Danny Gatton, and Brent Mason, among others, were often even cleaner and faster.

Concomitantly, rock 'n' roll and rockabilly gained footing, and over time infiltrated the somewhat staid Nashville culture. This cultural phenomenon most significantly expanded country music's instrumental parameters, manifesting itself not only in longer and more aggressive distorted guitar solos, but also in more powerful chord progressions extending beyond the genre's typical I–IV–V changes and 2/4 time signatures. By the 1980s, country music made the leap from honky tonks and the Opry to arenas and stadiums, starring black-hatted "cowboys" with sharp-shooting lead guitarists. Purists may have been given pause, but the effect has been one to give country music heretofore undreamed of popularity among a younger demographic while providing a smooth test track for Nashville cats to burn the windings off their strings.

About the CD

This book's accompanying audio CD includes all twenty-five solos performed note for note with a full band and is playable on any CD player. For PC and MAC computer users, the CD is enhanced with Amazing Slow Downer software so you can adjust the recording to any tempo without changing pitch!

The time code shown at the start of each solo transcription indicates the point at which the solo begins in the original recording.

All music on the CD performed by:
Guitar: Doug Boduch
Bass: Tom McGirr and Eric Hervey
Keyboards: Warren Wiegratz
Drums: Scott Schroedl

Recorded, mixed, and mastered by Jim Reith and Jake Johnson.

Contents

Merle Travis

Photo provided by Michael Ochs Archives/Getty Images

"Merle Travis could write you a hit song and sing it; he could draw you a cartoon, play you a great guitar solo, or fix your watch."

—Chet Atkins

In the mid-1940s, singer Jack "Tex" Williams and his band were playing polkas. But in 1947, guitarist Merle Travis co-wrote "Smoke, Smoke, Smoke (That Cigarette)" along with Williams, and the song became a #1 pop and country hit, as well as Capitol Records' first million seller. This success compelled Williams and his Western Caravan to change their musical style and embrace the trendy boogie-based numbers like "Smoke" that pre-figured rock 'n' roll and honky-tonk.

Like his protégé Chet Atkins, Merle Robert Travis was a giant of country guitar. Born November 29, 1917, in hardscrabble Rosewood, Kentucky, he started frailing 5-string banjo as a child before turning his prodigious talents to the guitar at the age of 12. His neighbors Ike Everly (father to brothers Don and Phil Everly) and Mose Rager tutored Travis in the three-finger right-hand style that would later become known as "Travis picking." From 1938–1941, as a member of the Drifting Pioneers, he appeared regularly on *Boone County Jamboree* on WLW radio in Cincinnati. He also performed with Grandpa Jones and the Delmore Brothers, with whom he made the first recordings for King Records.

After a brief tour of duty with the Marines during World War II, Travis returned to Cincinnati and made a number of "soundies"—the first music videos—before following his muse to Los Angeles, in 1944. He quickly found work in western movies, on radio, and in Ray Whitley's Western Swing band. In 1946 Travis signed with Capitol Records and released his first hit single, "No Vacancy" b/w "Cincinnati Lou." That same year he met luthier Paul Bigsby and had him build a solidbody electric guitar—one of the first solidbody electrics the world would see, and arguably the inspiration for Leo Fender's Stratocaster design (a charge Fender has always denied).

In 1947, on witnessing the success singer Burl Ives was having on the folk market, Capitol Records A&R man Lee Gillette had Travis record a set of four 78 RPM platters titled *Folk Songs of the Hills* in a misguided attempt to cash in on the phenomenon. Though the solo acoustic guitar project was a commercial failure, it did contain an influential group of future country classics including, "Sixteen Tons" and "Nine Pound Hammer." The unqualified success of "Smoke, Smoke, Smoke (That Cigarette)" later that year, however, gave Travis encouragement, as did the string of Top 10 hits like "So Round, So Firm, So Fully Packed," "Divorce Me C.O.D.," "Sweet Temptation," "Steel Guitar Rag," and "Fat Gal" that followed in the next five years. Another hit,

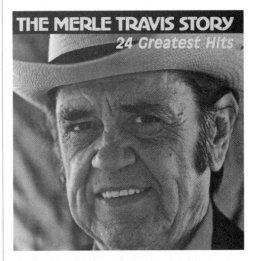

His rakish appearance on the cover is a fine indicator of Merle Travis's approach to the guitar on "Re-enlistment Blues," "Nine Pound Hammer," and the all-time classic "Steel Guitar Rag."

"Merle's Boogie Woogie," from 1951, is an early example of using a sped up track, thus predating Les Paul's noted use of the technique. Travis's appearance singing "Re-enlistment Blues" in 1953's *From Here to Eternity*—the first of 16 film appearances—gave his sagging career a boost, just as the film did for fading pop star Frank Sinatra. Recordings with his friend Hank Thompson, along with Tennessee Ernie Ford's hit version of "Sixteen Tons" in 1955 also contributed to his resurgence.

Despite his enormous talent and charisma, Travis could never sustain his success due to a severe drinking problem that resulted in numerous arrests, charges of spousal abuse, and eventually hospitalization in the early 1960s. Upon his release from the hospital, Travis moved to Nashville where he appeared at the Grand Ole Opry for a spell and resumed his recording career. *Walking on the Strings* revealed undiminished chops while his cameo with Mother Maybelle Carter on the Nitty Gritty Dirt Band's *Will the Circle Be Unbroken*, in 1971, lent credibility to the landmark recording. In 1974 he won a GRAMMY® for his *Atkins-Travis Traveling Show*, and his career enjoyed a fine "second act." In 1982 Travis resumed his film work, with Clint Eastwood in *Honky Tonk Man*, before his final curtain was drawn on October 20, 1983, following a heart attack.

How to Play It

In the song's second guitar solo, Merle Travis shares sixteen measures with guitarist Smokey Rogers, who burns with single-note lines in contrast to the syncopated chordal textures that precede his time in the spotlight. In a manner similar to his first eight-measure solo (earlier in the song), Travis does his "picking" over D9–A7–D9–B7–E9 changes. The secret to his justly lauded style lies first in the left-hand fingering, which regularly consists of a chord shape held in place with an occasional scale tone thrown in. As for his magnificent right-hand technique, Travis employs only his thumb and index finger in a marvelous display of rhythmic independence.

In measures 1–2, Travis stretches his pinky, middle, and index fingers, low to high, to form a D7 triple stop (minus the root, which is sounded on beat 4 of the previous measure), and the addition of the open high E string completes the D9 voicing. His right-hand approach in this section is an altered form of his famous Travis picking, where he alternates between strings 6 and 4 when playing solo guitar or accompaniment. In this solo he attacks strings 4 and 3 with his thumbpick while grabbing strings 2 and 1 with his index finger.

In measures 3–4, Travis forms an open position A7 chord minus the root, as adding bass root notes could potentially clash with the bassist. There are a couple of options for left-hand fingering in these two measures, but the middle and ring fingers, low to high, are a good, logical choice.

Travis applies the same left- and right-hand templates to measures 5–6 (D9) as in measures 1–2. Instead of the steady eighth-note flow of notes typical of the Travis style, however, observe the inclusion of more quarter notes, which contributes variety to the phrasing and rhythm of the solo. In addition, do not miss the brief modulation from F♯ to G on beat 4 of measure 6; this move functions to clarify the shift to B7 in measure 7, as it also is voiced with F♯ as the lowest note in the chord.

Once in measure 7, Travis barres strings 4–2 with his index finger at the fourth fret while adding his middle finger on string 1 at the fifth fret, to create a B7 chord. (Note: To avoid a position shift, you may also choose to form the fourth-fret barre with your ring finger and use your pinky finger on the top string at the fifth fret.) His choice of voicings makes for a slick change to the E7 triple stop (fingered middle–index–ring, low to high) that ends the solo in measure 8. Both moves are staples of blues repertoire and reflect Travis's deep blues roots.

In measures 9–16 Travis (Gtr. 1) graciously resorts to playing rhythm for Smokey Rogers (Gtr. 2), taking the opportunity to show off his thumbpicked alternating bass style. Meanwhile, Smokey craftily hiccups his way into a scintillating eighth-note line in Mixolydian mode, adding a tasty flat 3rd (C) for some bluesy color. Clearly no hack himself, Smokey Rogers was a fixture in the Western swing scene, playing with the likes of Bob Wills, Tex Williams, and Spade Cooley.

Vital Stats

Guitarist: Merle Travis

Song: "Smoke, Smoke, Smoke (That Cigarette)"

Album: *Merle Travis Story: 24 Greatest Hits*, 1989

Age at time of recording: 30

Guitar: 1946 Bigsby solidbody electric

1:50

Guitar Solo

Fast ♩ = 130

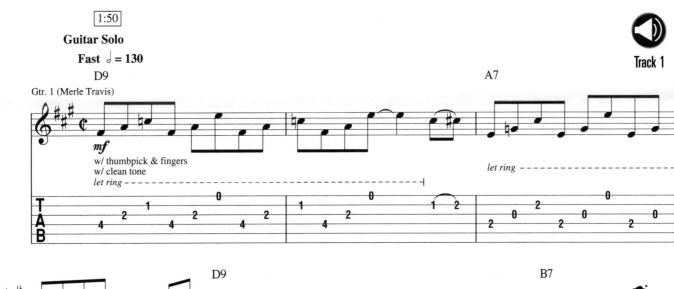

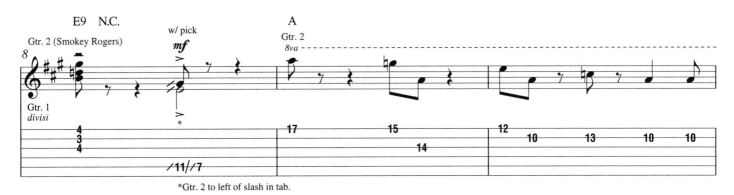

*Gtr. 2 to left of slash in tab.

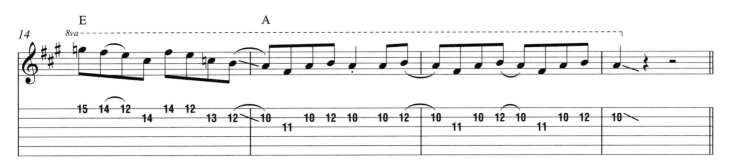

Words and Music by Merle Travis and Tex Williams
Copyright © 1947 by Unichappell Music Inc. and Elvis Presley Music
Copyright Renewed
All Rights Administered by Unichappell Music Inc.
International Copyright Secured   All Rights Reserved

3

Hank Garland

Courtesy R.A. Andreas/Cache Agency

Through the years, the careers of several country guitarists have been cut short, but few are as heartbreaking as that of Hank Garland. But before fate stilled his music he contributed significantly to the language of steaming country guitar and crossed over to the world of jazz like no one else before or since.

"Real nice. He never got upset about anything."

—Hank Garland
on recording with Elvis

Walter Louis "Hank" Garland was born in Cowpens, South Carolina, on November 11, 1930. Hearing "Wildwood Flower" performed by Mother Maybelle Carter on the radio in 1936 led to his getting a used acoustic from his father. Garland would eventually come under the spell of Arthur "Guitar Boogie" Smith, in 1938, when he heard the pioneering electric guitarist and made a subsequent attempt to electrify his own axe. In 1945, the 15-year old Garland was invited to appear at the Grand Ole Opry, where he brought the house down with a boogie instrumental. Opry star Paul Howard offered him a gig, but the musicians union refused him membership until he turned 16. By 1946 Garland was playing twin guitar parts in Howard's band before going off with Cowboy Copas for two years.

In 1949, Garland signed a contract with Decca Records in Nashville. The instru-

mental "Sugarfoot Rag" was released, and when Red Foley added lyrics and cut it later the same year with Garland reproducing his licks, it became a hit and garnered him the nickname "Sugarfoot." The young guitarist became enamored with the Gypsy guitar genius Django Reinhardt in the early 1950s while playing with future country music legend Eddy Arnold. Whenever Arnold's band would make sojourns to New York City, Garland would hit the jazz clubs and take lessons from jazz guitarist Barry Galbraith. In 1955 he co-designed a thin, short-scale hollow body guitar for Gibson with Billy Byrd that would later be called the Byrdland.

In the mid-1950s, Garland played in a number of jazz and pop combos while immersing himself in Nashville session work as a member of the "A-Team." From 1957–61, he regularly backed Elvis Presley, playing on the #1 hits "Are You Lonesome Tonight?" "Stuck on You," "It's Now or Never," "Surrender," "Can't Help Falling in Love," "Crying in the Chapel," "His Latest Flame," and "A Big Hunk O'

Mr. "Sugarfoot" could play it sweet or tart as evidenced by this potluck musical repast with the jazz of "Sentimental Journey," the pop movie hit "The Third Man Theme," and the rocking "E-String Rag," among other tasty delights.

Love." In addition, his versatile, tasty, and commanding chops allowed him to moonlight on other rock 'n' roll records such as the Everly Brothers' "Bye Bye Love" and Bobby Helm's "Jingle Bell Rock."

Despite having a contract specifying that he play only "country music," Garland finally got his chance to "blow" some jazz in 1960, recording with vibist Gary Burton, bassist Joe Benjamin, and drummer Joe Morello from Dave Brubeck's band. The resulting and prophetically titled *Jazz Winds from a New Direction* became a landmark album, appealing to both jazz and progressive country music fans. In 1961, however, he was back in the stultifying session scene and backing Presley on "Little Sister" and at his farewell concert in Hawaii. Tragedy struck in September of that year, however, when following a fight with his wife, Evelyn, and thinking she had left with his kids for Milwaukee, Garland sped off after her and was involved in a serious accident that left him in a coma.

He awoke weeks later only to find that his brain injury had robbed him of most of his coordination and concentration. As a result, Garland could play guitar for only brief periods of time and was thus unable to continue his career. He and his family then moved to Milwaukee, where Evelyn ironically died in a car accident in 1963. In 1975, Garland appeared at the Fan Fair Reunion Show at the Opry and heroically played "Sugarfoot Rag." He spent his last years living with his sister and her husband before dying on December 27, 2004. A biopic was released in 2006 starring Wayne Payne as Garland, and Steve Vai (!) as Hank Williams, Sr.

How to Play It

The sixteen-measure solo consists of four four-bar sections. Measures 1–4, 9–12, and 13–16 follow A–E–A chord changes, while measures 5–8 get a Mixolydian tonality with its A–G–A–E–A progression. As such, Garland improvises in clearly defined four-measure phrases that complement the "country" syncopation of the music, while at the same time avoiding the temptation to simply burn nonstop through the phrases with rapidly picked lines.

Right out of the chute Garland flashes jagged bends in the A hybrid blues scale (blues scale plus Mixolydian mode), which in turn create musical tension. He bounces off that tension with ascending runs in measure 3 that deliberately resolve to A notes in measure 4. Check out how after the classic blues hammer-on from C to C# (b3rd–3rd) on beat 2 of measure 3, Garland introduces the first of several legato trill moves that recurs throughout the short solo.

In measures 5–6, Garland maps the chord changes by first playing a run using the notes from an A9 chord, and then following it up with the exact same pattern two frets lower, using notes from a G9 chord. Also be aware of the trills on beat 3 of each measure, a somewhat rare occurrence in country guitar of the late 1940s era. Further, his crafty legato attack produces a "swoosh" that adds dynamic contrast to all the picked notes. In measures 7–8, Garland follows with a brisk run down the A composite scale that contains a similar legato trill on beat

3 of measure 8 before resolving cleanly to the tonic A note.

Garland next relocates to second position, in measures 9–12, for some deep-chest tones along with a bunch of relatively slower quarter notes to provide contrast to the preceding eight measures. The phrasing here is more "down home" and might sound a bit like chicken pickin' if it was faster. Observe how he builds this four-bar motif on the A note on string 3 at fret 2 and the F# note on string 4 at fret 4, for a completely different sound all around. In doing so, Garland creates some slight tension that eventually resolves to the tonic A in measure 12.

In measures 13–14, Garland revisits the legato "swoosh" motif in a manner similar to measures 5–6, with the difference being that the legato riff is repeated and rhythmically displaced to different beats. The F# slipped in between the trills provides some hefty musical tension that resolves to the bluegrass-style ascending run in the A composite blues scale in measures 15–16.

Vital Stats

Guitarist: Hank Garland

Song: "Sugarfoot Rag"

Album: *Hank Garland & His Sugar Footers*, 1992

Age at time of recording: 19

Guitar: 1940s Epiphone Zephyr

Amp: 1940s Gibson EH-150

Sugarfoot Rag

1:21

Guitar Solo
Fast Country Two-step ♩ = 124

Track 2

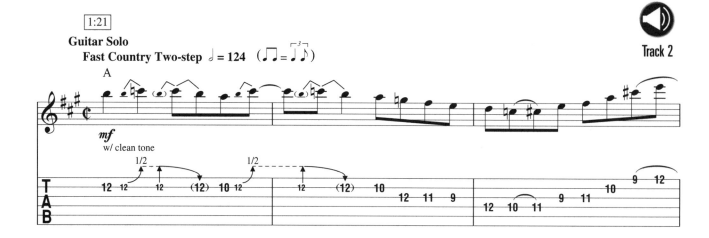

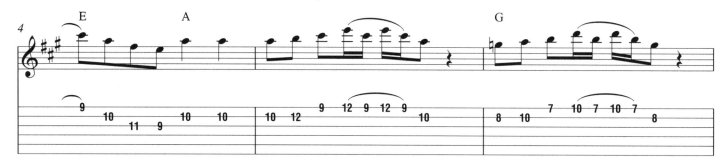

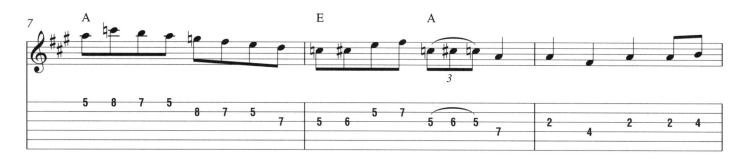

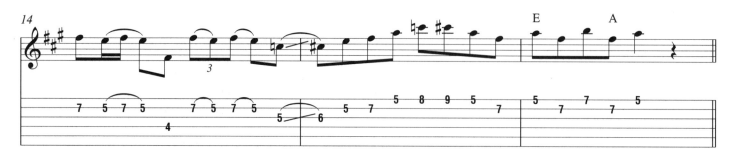

Words and Music by Hank Garland and Vaughn Horton
TRO - © Copyright 1949 (Renewed) and 1950 (Renewed) Cromwell Music, Inc. and Hollis Music, Inc., New York, NY
International Copyright Secured
All Rights Reserved Including Public Performance For Profit
Used by Permission

Hank Snow

Canada isn't normally thought of as a hotbed for country music, but Canadian guitarist Hank Snow traversed both literal and figurative miles to reach the heart of country music. Along the way he left a legacy of road music that reverberates all the way to present day across all genres, including rock 'n' roll.

Clarence Eugene Snow was born in Brooklyn, Nova Scotia, on May 9, 1914. When he was eight, he went to live with his grandmother following the divorce of his parents. She was an abusive woman, and the experience would scar Snow's childhood and eventually result in the grand theme of his music. When his mother remarried four years later he rejoined her but unfortunately encountered abuse from her new husband. This new arrangement soon became intolerable, compelling Snow to run away at the age of 12. He then became a cabin boy on a fishing boat, where he would often sing to the crew's delight.

Snow returned home at 16, in 1930, and was given a stack of Jimmie Rodgers records by his mother, along with rudimentary lessons on a cheap mail-order guitar she had acquired. Snow applied himself and before long began to develop his own style while playing for friends and neighbors. By 1933 he was good

"'Hank' sounds more Western than 'Clarence.'"

—Suggested to Snow by Cecil Landry of Canadian radio station CHNS in 1934

enough to go to Halifax, Nova Scotia, and appear on a radio show called "Down on the Farm" as either the Cowboy Blue Yodeler or Clarence Snow and his Guitar before it was suggested by the station manager he change his name to "Hank" for a more authentic handle. In 1936 he signed with RCA's Bluebird label in Montreal and released "The Prisoned Cowboy" and "Lonesome Blue Yodel," both of which became hits above the border while demonstrating his musical debt to the yodeling Rodgers. Over the next ten years, Snow would wax more then ninety singles for the label while keeping his eye on the prize he yearned to seize in the U.S.

During World War II, Snow unsuccessfully tried to break into the U.S. market, often performing with his trick pony Shawnee, as RCA steadfastly refused to release his records in the U.S. until he had a solid following. His timing was also bad, as the American public was understandably distracted by the war. Then, in 1948, he was singing on the Big D Jamboree in Dallas, where a friendship with country artist Ernest Tubb led to a slot at the Grand Ole Opry in early 1950. To his good fortune, Snow's appearance in Nashville's hallowed hall coincided with RCA's finally acknowledging his commercial potential in the U.S. His first domestic single, "Marriage Vow," which was released in 1949, became a modest hit. But the phenomenal success

Photo provided by Photofest

Like virtually all the great pioneers of country guitar, Hank Snow could pick it pretty or peppy, with equal understatement, in all the popular styles. "The Gal Who Invented Kissin'" and "Hello Love" are balanced out by "The Rhumba Boogie" and the landmark "I'm Movin' On."

of "I'm Moving On" (1950) dispelled any lingering doubts about Snow's marketability, as it shot to #1 on the country charts and remained there for an astounding twenty-one weeks—still a record. In 1951, "Golden Rocket" and "The Rhumba Boogie" also went to the top of the charts. Along with a knack for writing catchy, driving songs, Snow displayed an effective guitar style, its greatest strength being its unadorned, graceful simplicity.

Snow returned the favor of getting into the Grand Ole Opry by pushing for Elvis Presley to appear, in 1954; he was also instrumental in getting Presley to sign with RCA. Indeed, Snow had formed a booking agency with the soon to be notorious Col. Tom Parker, Presley's new manager, but he would later come to regret the ruthless Parker's involvement with the "King" and his abandonment of country music for rock 'n' roll. Snow became a U.S. citizen in 1958 and then lived in the country Top 10 until 1965, occasionally experimenting with "light" rock 'n' roll along the way. In the late 1960s he was still a popular performer, but his traditional-sounding records were out of sync with the new Nashville and Bakersfield styles, and sales suffered. His last big hit, "Hello Love," went to #1 in 1974, when he was 61. Despite being inducted into the Nashville Songwriters Hall of Fame, in 1978, and the Country Music Hall of Fame a year later, RCA unceremoniously dropped him from their roster in 1981—after seventy million records sold and forty-seven continuous years with the label, yet another record. Snow remained active in the Opry until 1996, before dying on December 20, 1999, from respiratory failure.

How to Play It

Hank Snow lets his big, unamplified Martin guitar do the talking over a typical sixteen-measure country chorus of E, A, and B7 chord changes. Coming at a time when the electric guitar as a solo voice was starting to command attention in the genre (especially through Chet Atkins), it was a reminder of country music's prewar roots as well as a potent symbol of the timeless power of vibrant acoustic steel strings and the natural resonance of wood.

In measures 1–2, Snow mixes open strings with the E tonality-defining double stop of B/G♯, to produce an appropriate harmony that makes up for the lack of another chordal instrument behind him—an approach he applies throughout. Check out the double stop of C♯/B on beat 1 of measure 2. The implied E6 tonality expands the harmony beyond the usual triad. Snow smartly navigates the change to A in measure 3 by sliding into an E/C♯ (5th/3rd) double stop, followed by the open A string. The open E notes that follow offer a smooth transition into measure 4, where the top two strings played open connect logically back to the E chord in measure 5. Note how the half-step bend of F♯ to G in measure 4 implies an A7 tonality to precede and lead into the E chord in measure 5. Far from being a programmatic guitarist, though, Snow mixes up his musical "tools" in measure 5, where he uses the most minimal means—the B note at fret 4 on string 3, combined with the open B and E strings—to forge a strong, basic E tonality.

Like any guitarist responsible for marking chord changes, Snow inserts harmony where necessary, using various inversions to keep things lively. *Inversions* are chord voicings in which a note other than the root is on the bottom. A first-inversion voicing has the 3rd of the chord as the lowest note, and a second-inversion voicing has the 5th in the bass. Exhibit one in the "Golden Rocket" solo is the second-inversion E major triad on beat 1 of measure 6. Maintaining the concept, he plays a first-inversion B major triad in measure 7 along with an unusual and bluesy Badd9 triple stop in measure 8.

Measures 9–13 are similar to measure 1–5 as a compositional device to provide structure and coherence to the solo by repeating certain licks as a motif. An exception, however, occurs in measure 10 where Snow plays D/G♯ to imply E7. Seventh chords function to lead the ear to the next chord change, in this case, A, in measure 11. Snow takes the "Golden Rocket" home in measures 14–16 by comping the chord changes with propulsive strumming to connect the solo back to verse 4.

Vital Stats

Guitarist: Hank Snow

Song: "Golden Rocket"

Album: *Essential Hank Snow,* 1997

Age at time of recording: 36

Guitar: 1934 Martin D-28

2:00

Guitar Solo
Fast Country Two-step ♩ = 120

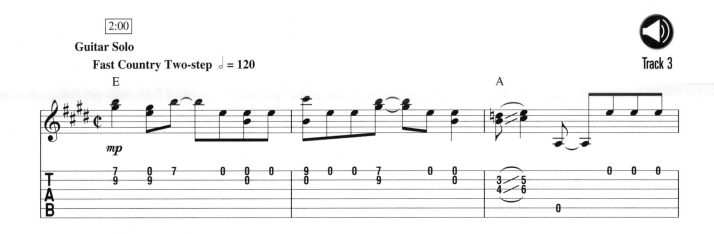

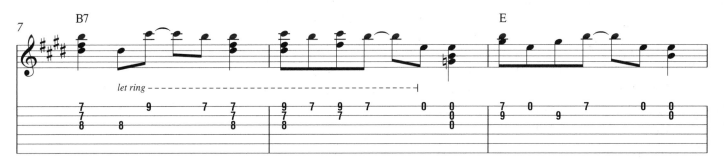

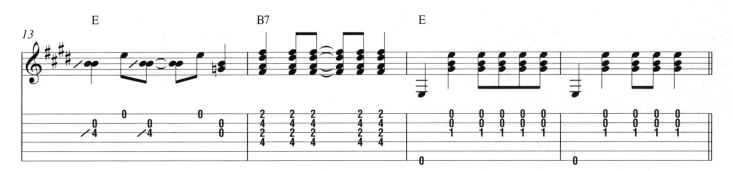

Words and Music by Hank Snow
Copyright © 1950 by Unichappell Music Inc.
Copyright Renewed
International Copyright Secured   All Rights Reserved

Chet Atkins

"I'd like for people to say I played in tune, that I played in good taste, and that I was nice to people."

—Chet Atkins

Of all the illustrious "hillbillies" who ever climbed off a hay wagon to pick a guitar, Chet Atkins tops the list. "Mr. Guitar" was a pervasive influence in Nashville and beyond for nigh on fifty years. From his unsurpassed Travis-style fingerpicking—which he developed to the point where he could play "Yankee Doodle" and "The Battle Hymn of the Republic" at the *same* time—to his

pioneering use of a proto-wah pedal ("Boo Boo Stick Beat") and subtle Bigsby bar flourishes, Atkins proclaimed an unending love affair with the guitar.

Chester Burton Atkins was born in Luttrell, Tennessee, on June 20, 1924. His father was a piano teacher and singing evangelist, though it was Atkins' guitar-playing older half-brother Jim who would turn out to be his main inspiration. Initially, the younger Atkins began playing the fiddle. He then acquired his first guitar at age nine, when he swapped one for a pistol. Soon afterwards Mother Maybelle Carter, George Barnes, Karl Farr from the Sons of the Pioneers, Django Reinhardt, Les Paul, and especially Merle Travis came into his life through the radio speakers and left a lasting impression.

By 1941 Atkins was a skilled enough axeman to audition at Knoxville's KNOX radio station to play on the *Bill Carlisle Show*. He was hired, but it was to play fiddle instead of guitar. In 1946 he made his first appearance at the Grand Ole Opry, with Red Foley, and later that year recorded for Bullet Records. But his big break came when, upon hearing a demo tape of Atkins' playing, RCA Victor's country music honcho Steve Sholes tracked down Atkins, hoping he could do for RCA what Merle Travis was doing for Capitol Records. Sholes and RCA were sufficiently impressed with Atkins' playing to install him as the studio guitarist for all Nashville sessions, in 1949.

Atkins' next break came when he joined Mother Maybelle and the Carter Sisters as the regular

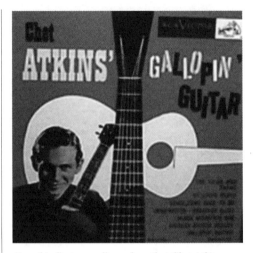

Even his first recordings show that Chet Atkins was so musical and adept on the guitar that he probably could have made scale exercises compelling.

guitarist on the Grand Ole Opry, in 1950. As *the* guitar man, he recorded with most of the genre's stars, and in 1953 RCA made him a consultant. Meanwhile, he also was afforded the opportunity to record instrumentals like his signature "Country Gentleman," in 1953, and two certifiable hits, "Mr. Sandman" and "Silver Bell," with Hank Snow, in 1955. He went on to have his own radio show on Nashville's WSM radio, an endorsement with Gretsch Guitars, an instruction course, and a home studio.

In 1957 Atkins was made manager of the RCA Nashville division, where he produced records for Elvis Presley, Eddy Arnold, Hank Snow, Jim Reeves, and Don Gibson, whose "Oh Lonesome Me" b/w "I Can't Stop Loving You" (1958) is considered a Nashville landmark. In the 1960s he played the Newport Jazz Festival and at the White House, for President John F. Kennedy. In 1965 he had a country and pop crossover hit with "Yakety Axe"—a guitar version of Boots Randolph's "Yakety Sax"—and lastly with a remake of "Country Gentleman," in 1969.

The 1970s found Chet still recording regularly but with diminished enthusiasm, due to RCA's reluctance to give him the go-ahead for a jazz album. In

Photo provided by Photofest

1975, however, he teamed with long-time idol and friend Les Paul—recording as Chester and Lester—for a gorgeous set of jazz and pop standards spiced with their witty repartee. In addition, he also recorded with the doomed Canadian virtuoso Lenny Breau, as well as Jerry Reed, Doc Watson, and Merle Travis. In 1977 Atkins severed his endorsement with Gretsch, in favor of Gibson.

By 1982 his ties with RCA had also been stretched to the point of breaking, and he did the previously unthinkable, signing with Columbia Records. In 1983 he began referring to himself as "Chet Atkins, C.G.P.," with the initials standing for "Certified Guitar Player." With his newfound creative freedom he indulged his penchant for pop and jazz in a series of records made with Mark Knopfler (Dire Straits) and Jerry Reed, in the 1990s, along with recordings featuring jazz-fusion guitarists George Benson, Larry Carlton, and Earl Klugh.

Atkins' health declined in his final years, but he survived long enough to witness the unveiling of a life-size bronze statue of "Mr. Guitar" in Nashville, in 2001. He died of cancer just a short time later, on June 30, 2001. His fourteen GRAMMY® Awards and nine Country Music Association Awards for Musician of the Year, among countless other honors, assure his standing as one of the greatest guitarists of all time, in any genre.

How to Play It

Tommy Dorsey was the first to record "Chinatown, My Chinatown," at the onset of the swing era, in 1935. When Chet Atkins included it on his 1953 debut album, *Chet Atkins' Gallopin' Guitar*, it helped signal Nashville's embrace of pop music as a commercially viable influence.

Atkins' instrumental version, with only upright bass for accompaniment, contains five thirty-two-measure sections given alphabetical designations known as rehearsal letters. In letters A–D Atkins either states the vocal melody with accuracy or invents subtle variations with mostly chordal forms. Upon reaching rehearsal letter E, however, Atkins breaks out with what amounts to more of an improvised solo, with many brisk single-note lines that ring "clean as country water." A major component of his immaculate technique can be found in his right-hand approach. Atkins played fingerstyle, using his bare index, middle, and ring fingers, with his pinky lightly anchored to the top of his guitar, and a plastic thumbpick in place. The thumbpick was chiefly employed on the bass strings, which were more often than not palm-muted for a percussive effect that contrasted dynamically with his brightly ringing treble strings. That being said, he was not adverse to strumming and picking single notes with it as if it were a flat pick.

In the grand jazz tradition of using the melody as a jumping off point, Atkins starts with parallel sliding 5ths in measures 1–4, evoking the popular notion of Chinese music, as well as suggesting the first vocal line of the tune. Following in measures 5–8 is a brilliant flash of harmony that only Atkins would likely envision in 1953. A descending pattern of sweet, warm 6ths, from fret 12 to fret 7, bridges the A–E7 chord change, while simultaneously acknowledging the melody and making a smooth transition to the bracing single notes to come.

Observe that it would be most efficient to barre across strings 3–1 with your index finger all the way down, using either your ring or middle finger for the hammer-ons on string 3.

Measures 9–13 find Atkins in the E major scale displaying considerable speed, a skill that he only trotted out on occasion, even as he adheres to the changes by hitting notes relative to the C#7 and F#m chords. Be aware that he literally slips his left hand into an F#m barre chord for measures 12–13 in a typical move. In measures 14 and 16 he dips his Bigsby whammy bar in his slinky, sensual trademark style. Even cooler is the "trick" in measure 22, where he depresses the bar one full step before striking the 7th fret note and releasing the bar to bring the pitch back up to F#.

Like many other great postwar country guitarists, Atkins had a love for jazz that manifested itself in many ways, including the slick octaves in measures 17–21 that would make George Benson proud, not to mention Wes Montgomery and Django Reinhardt. To put the cherry on top of his sumptuous creation, he ends with a hip, softly pulsing A6/9 chord.

Vital Stats

Guitarist: Chet Atkins

Song: "Chinatown, My Chinatown"

Album: *Chet Atkins Gallopin' Guitar*, 1953

Age at time of recording: 29

Guitar: 1954 Gretsch 6192 Country Club

Amp: Butts Echosonic

11

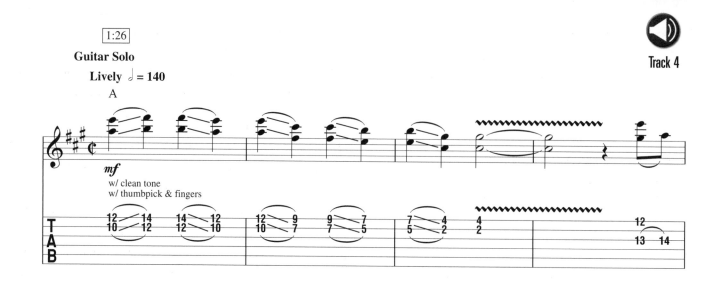

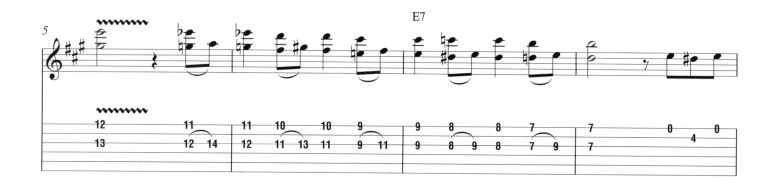

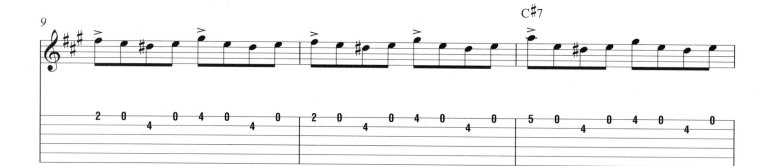

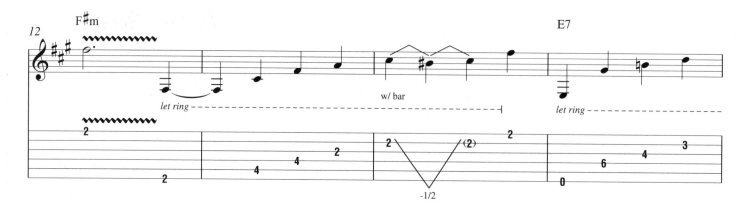

12

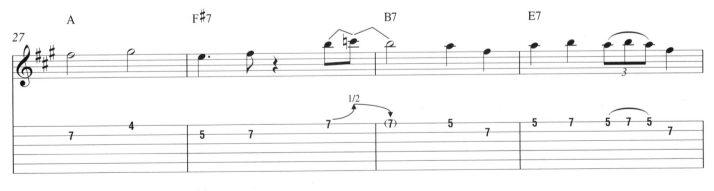

Lester Flatt

Together, banjoist Earl Scruggs and guitarist Lester Flatt were likely the greatest and most popular exponents of bluegrass music to come down the pike. With Scruggs' high-energy, flat-out, virtuosic picking and Flatt's propulsive comping, bass lines, and idiomatic runs, they made hillbilly music far above and beyond what the father of bluegrass, Bill Monroe, could ever have envisioned. Both instrumentalists made revolutionary contributions to the genre— Scruggs with his three-finger banjo-picking style and Flatt's now eponymous flatpicking run in G—that continue to influence contemporary players.

Lester Raymond Flatt was born on June 19, 1914, near Sparta, Tennessee. His father attempted to teach him banjo, but the young Flatt could not master the drop-thumb technique and so instead began playing guitar and singing in the church choir. By the age of 10 he was attracting recognition for his skills. As a teenager and then through the 1930s, he worked a series of mill jobs in North Carolina and Tennessee. When Flatt and his wife, Gladys, relocated to Roanoke,

Photo provided by Michael Ochs Archives/Getty Images

As it was his first instrument, Lester Flatt may have played "second fiddle" to Earl Scruggs, but his nimble runs are second to none on "Shuckin' the Corn," "Randy Lynn Rag," and "Foggy Mountain Chimes."

Virginia, in 1935, Flatt joined Charlie Scott's Harmonizers and appeared with them on radio station WDBJ. When rheumatoid arthritis forced Flatt to quit mill work, it presented the perfect opportunity for him to give his musical career a go.

The Flatts moved to Burlington, North Carolina, in 1940, where Lester found a raft of musical opportunities with various country outfits. Joining Charlie Monroe in his Kentucky Pardners, in 1943, would prove the gateway to future success. Flatt first played mandolin along side guitarist Monroe but eventually developed his signature guitar style, playing the bass strings with a plastic

"He was a powerful man in bluegrass music."
—Bill Monroe

thumbpick and raking up on the top strings with a steel index finger pick for chordal forms. When Flatt left the Kentucky Pardners, Bill Monroe— Charlie's brother and the acknowledged father of bluegrass music—offered him the position of playing rhythm guitar and singing lead with his Blue Grass Boys. The group debuted at the Grand Ole Opry in March of 1945, and by Christmas of that year, Earl Scruggs had also joined what would become arguably the first and greatest bluegrass group of all time.

The band was on the road constantly, and it took its toll on all the members as both Scruggs and Flatt quit in 1948. In short order they gathered other Monroe alumni and formed Lester Flatt, Earl Scruggs, and the Foggy Mountain Boys. They would play together for the next 21 years, in the process changing the face of country music with songs like their signature "Foggy Mountain Breakdown" that showcased Scruggs' and the band's virtuosity. Such was their popularity that they weathered the various changes in country music in the 1950s and 1960s, and from 1959–68 they accumulated 40 Top 10 singles. In 1962 they peaked with their "Ballad of Jed Clampett," the theme song for the hit TV show "The Beverly Hillbillies," on which they made several cameo appearances. In 1963 the song became the first bluegrass ditty to reach #1 on the country charts. In 1964 they also recorded the theme for the TV show "Petticoat Junction," and in 1968 saw "Foggy Mountain Breakdown" prominently played in the movie *Bonnie & Clyde*. The group also won a GRAMMY® for the album *Original Foggy Mountain Breakdown*.

In 1969 the duo split over artistic differences as Scruggs went in a more progressive direction with his son in the Earl Scruggs Revue, while Flatt stayed the course in the Nashville Grass. Both bands achieved a fair degree of success, and Flatt added 12-year old Marty Stuart to his band in 1972. A reunion of Scruggs and Flatt was planned in 1979, but it was thwarted when Flatt became ill, and then died a short while later, on May 11.

How to Play It

"Foggy Mountain Special" is a 12-bar blues disguised as a bluegrass song, in cut time. Though nowhere near as prevalent in contemporary country music, which borrows so heavily from pop and rock sources, there was a time when the "two-beat" was the typical feel, especially in bluegrass music. One of its effects is that a great deal of dynamic tension is produced when fast picking is overlaid the rather stately and sedate cut time signature. In addition, because the measures appear to go by twice as fast, the whole notes as in measures 2, 5, 9, and 12 also add dynamic contrast to the other measures without losing the forward momentum of the solo.

In this tune, all of Lester's strings are tuned up a half step (from low to high: E#–A#–D#–G#–B#–E#). In the early days of Flatt & Scruggs, both Lester and Earl tuned up a half step to accommodate Lester's vocal range. This way they could avoid using a capo. However, to play along with the recording, you can use a capo at the first fret, or tune up like Lester did.

Measures 1, 3, 7, and 11 contain Flatt's classic "G run" in all its glory. It is derived from the G major-blues scale (1–2–b3–3–5–6), which is simply the major pentatonic scale with an added b3rd degree. Here, the b3rd (Bb) on string 5 at fret 1 functions as a bluesy passing tone to the B. Be sure to pick up on the feel of the run; the phrasing has a lilt and swing to it that is precise without being stiff. To play it most efficiently, try this picking pattern from low to high: Down, down, up, hammer-on, up, down, pull-off, and down. Though Flatt employed a thumbpick and an index finger–pick on his right hand, it is likely that he could have used just the thumbpick for the run. In any case, a flat pick will work just dandy.

Flatt & Scruggs began as a duo and vestiges of being the lone accompanist to the banjo king's nonstop picking remained in the guitarist's style. In "Foggy Mountain Special," it shows in the way Flatt strums C7 chords in measure 5 and D triads in measure 10, to complement the runs and contribute to the impression of him playing both the rhythm and lead parts simultaneously. Be sure to notice that for the C and D changes he reverses the approach he used for the G chord by playing the root note in the measure prior, as opposed to the measure afterwards, as he did for the G runs. The result adds variety and a change of dynamics that is welcome in this elegantly simple solo.

Vital Stats

Guitarist: Lester Flatt

Song: "Foggy Mountain Special"

Album: *Foggy Mountain Jamboree* – Flatt & Scruggs, 1957

Age at time of recording: 40

Guitar: 1950 Martin D-28

Foggy Mountain Special

Tune up 1/2 step:
(low to high) E#-A#-D#-G#-B#-E#

1:19

Guitar Solo

Moderately fast ♩ = 110

mf

w/ thumbpick & fingers

By Anne Louise Scruggs and Gladys Stacey Flatt
Copyright © 1954 UNIVERSAL - CEDARWOOD PUBLISHING
Copyright Renewed
All Rights Reserved   Used by Permission

Jimmy Bryant

"Of all the guitar players I have known, Jimmy Bryant is the fastest and the cleanest and has more technique than any other."

——Barney Kessel

Courtesy R.A. Andreas/Cache Agency

The heavyweight champ of "take-off" guitar, Jimmy Bryant was the first hot Tele picker and may have invented chicken pickin' with his "Pickin' the Chicken," in 1953. Though his playing was reined in and subdued when backing Nashville stars like Tennessee Ernie Ford in the 1950s, Bryant, along with his pedal steel counterpart Speedy West, would burn down the instrumental barn when left to his own devices in the studio.

John Ivy Bryant, Jr. was born on March 5, 1925, in Moultrie, Georgia. Like his fellow fret wizard Joe Maphis, Bryant first played the fiddle. Unlike Maphis, however, Bryant was locked in his room or beaten by his father if he did not practice, and he often ran away from home, once playing with Hank Williams as Little Fiddlin' Junior. At age 18 he finally escaped his home for good when he was drafted into the Army, in 1943. He was seriously wounded by a grenade in Germany and was sent to recuperate in a hospital in Washington, D.C., where he met and came under the influence of jazz guitarist Tony Mottola. Months in rehab spent listening to Gypsy jazz guitar great Django Reinhardt gave Bryant the chance to transfer his fiddle chops to the guitar, and upon his discharge he began

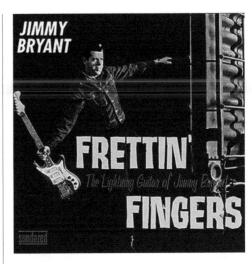

It has been said that a great actor could read the telephone book and make it dramatic, and likewise Jimmy Bryant could play a polka and make it hot—as he does on "Red Headed Polka."

playing jazz around the D.C. under the moniker "Buddy" Bryant.

In 1948 Bryant moved to southern California, where his virtuosity landed him a plum gig as lead, or "take-off" guitarist, with bassist, promoter, and Capitol Records A&R man Cliffie Stone, on his *Hometown Jamboree* radio and television broadcasts. In addition, the handsome and brash young Bryant found work as an extra in westerns, including three with Roy Rogers. Around 1949, Bryant met and forged a lasting musical partnership with Speedy West who had joined Stone's band.

In 1950, Leo Fender brought his serial number 1 Broadcaster guitar (forerunner of the Telecaster) to the Riverside Ranchero Club, where Bryant was "slumming." He enthusiastically embraced the innovative instrument, and Fender inked him to an endorsement deal and presented him with the historic axe as a gift. Their relationship would last for years, with only a minor interruption around 1953, when Bryant expected Fender to name his new, futuristic three-pickup guitar the "Jimmy Bryant

Model." Fender would instead call it the Stratocaster.

When country singer Tex Williams heard West and Bryant on the radio, he enlisted them to go into the Capitol Records studio with him and cut "Wild Card." Capitol then booked Bryant in 1951 to record "Bryant's Boogie," while changing his name from "Buddy" to "Jimmy." Later in the year West and Bryant cut "T-Bone Rag" and "Liberty Bell Polka," which were followed by more than fifty virtuosic instrumental tracks produced through 1960.

Like too many other exceptionally talented artists, Bryant was proud and a heavy drinker who often refused to "play down" and "turn down," resulting in his firing from the Jamboree in 1955. Capitol Records released his solo debut, *Country Cabin Jazz*, in 1960, though his contract with them had expired in 1956. He began doing sessions for Imperial along with releasing *The Fastest Guitar in the Country* and the instructional *Play Guitar with Jimmy Bryant* in 1967.

In 1970 Bryant moved to Las Vegas, but he returned to Georgia in 1974. The following year, he and West reunited to record an album in Nashville (released in 1990 as *For the Last Time*), and he relocated there in 1976, but he did not fit in with the conservative music scene. In 1979 it was revealed that he had terminal lung cancer, and he died on September 22, 1980, in Moultrie, Georgia. Speedy West died on November 15, 2003.

How to Play It

Jimmy Bryant is still regarded with awe as the original Master of the Telecaster. "Stratosphere Boogie," however, was performed on an unusual guitar called the Stratosphere, hence the title. Bryant had a financial interest in the Stratosphere Guitar Company of Springfield, Missouri, circa 1954, and played a Twin model with 6- and 12-string necks when he was on the outs with Leo Fender. He used the 6-string neck for his solo, but played other sections of the song on the 12-string neck, which was tuned in major and minor 3rds, creating spectacular ready-made harmony lines. The company only built approximately 200 guitars and was out of business by 1958.

Bryant's twenty-four-measure solo consists of two 12-bar choruses in B. He employs both the major scale and the composite blues scale (blues scale plus Mixolydian mode), with a few chromatic passages, to add the fluidity that was a hallmark of his improvisations. In measures 1–4 he works the B major scale starting with the root on string 5 at fret 14. Observe the consummate ease with which he gracefully and quickly ascends the scale for two measures and then descends for two measures to establish the solo's characteristic ebb and flow. For example, in measure 5 he transitions to the IV chord (E7) with a half-step move to the E composite blues scale on beat 1, and then ascends the contour through measure 6. He keeps the musical tension on high by remaining in the upper register for the return to the I (B) chord in measures 7–8. Bryant literally changes direction by flipping through a hip F#13/E (fingered like an Emaj7

arpeggio) in measure 9. Likewise, be sure to see how he repeats F# and A# (5th and ♭7th of B) in measures 11–12 like a honking horn player to drive home the tonality, while also creating musical tension heading into his second chorus.

In his second chorus, Bryant scorches his way to the conclusion. Notice the extremely snappy and clean hammer-ons and pull-offs scattered throughout. In measures 12–15 he whips through licks around the 7th position that, like most of the rest of the solo, tend to be very linear. Check out how Bryant again transitions skillfully between measures 15 and 16 with a pull-off from G# to F#, which are found in both the B and E major scales. Similarly, he uses the same two notes, only an octave lower, to make his move back to the I chord (B) in measure 19.

As one would expect from a guitar hero like Bryant, he does not disappoint in the stratospheric climax of this boogie. Starting on the root note (B) in measure 22, he zips through a chromatic line on strings 3 and 2 before resolving briefly to the root on string 1. Rather than halt this barreling momentum, Bryant keeps the listener's interest piqued through measure 24 with a sassy blues-bopper lick that any jazzer would be proud to call his own.

Vital Stats

Guitarist: Jimmy Bryant

Song: "Stratosphere Boogie"

Album: *Frettin' Fingers: The Lightning Guitar of Jimmy Bryant*, 2003

Age at time of recording: 29

Guitar: 1953 Stratosphere Twin 6/12 solidbody electric

Amp: Late 1940s wooden Fender Professional Amp

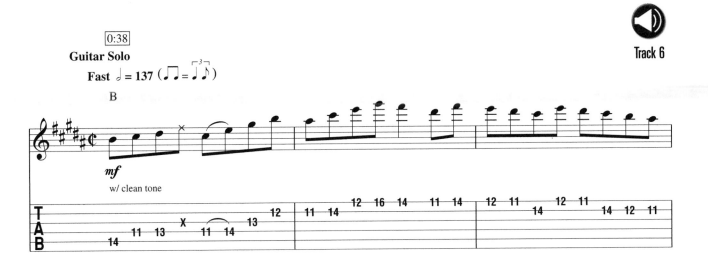

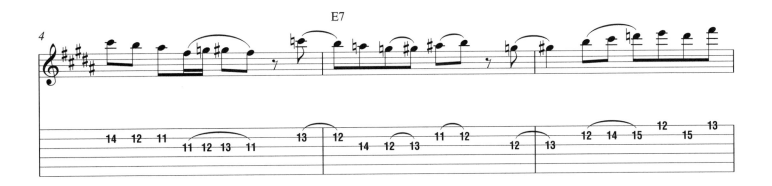

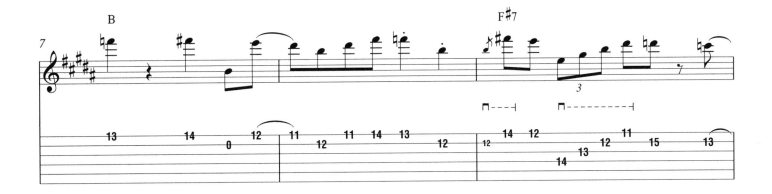

Words and Music by Jimmy Bryant
© 1954 (Renewed 1982) BEECHWOOD MUSIC CORP.

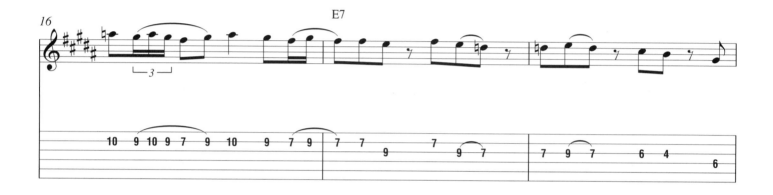

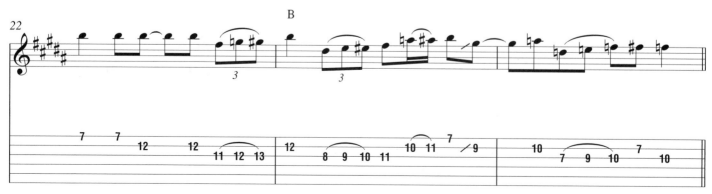

Joe Maphis

With a respectful nod to his equally combustible contemporary Jimmy Bryant, the hottest flat-picking country guitar begins with Joe "King of the Strings" Maphis. Acknowledged as the first to arrange fiddle tunes for the guitar, Maphis developed amazingly quick, crisp licks and did not depend on sustain or volume from amplification to enhance his stunning fluidity. A truly unsung guitar hero, Maphis could outgun all comers and make it look easy.

Otis Wilson Maphis was born on May 12, 1921, in Suffolk, Virginia. He was initially influenced by Mother Maybelle Carter and began playing the fiddle and the piano as a child, but soon focused his attention on a variety of stringed instruments, including the mandolin, tenor and 5-string banjo, upright bass, and guitar. In 1932, playing piano and guitar, Maphis joined his father in the Railsplitters and went on to perform on radio shows in Wheeling, West Virginia, on WLW in Cincinnati, and WLS in Chicago, Illinois while steadily building his reputation as a noteworthy picker.

"I'll never forget… 'Arkansas Traveler.' Here was the flawless, lightning-like execution of a master."

—Merle Travis on hearing Maphis on the radio for the first time

Photo provided by Michael Ochs Archives/Getty Images

During World War II, Maphis entertained the troops in the South Pacific, and after his discharge he started playing electric guitar, in 1947, and became a regular on the Old Dominion Barn Dance on WRVR radio in Richmond, Virginia. During his six-year stint on the show he met his future life partner in singer and guitarist Rose Lee in 1948. With sage advice from Merle Travis, the couple went to California in 1951, where more progressive country music was encouraged in Bakersfield. While there, Maphis would also become a sought-after session man on rockabilly and rock 'n' roll records. He and Lee married in 1952, and following the growing popularity of television in the early 1950s, they joined the Town Hall Party Show in Los Angeles for ten years. They also signed with Okeh Records, the R&B subsidiary of Columbia, waxing the biggest hit of their careers, "Dim Lights, Thick Smoke (And Loud, Loud Music)" in 1953. The couple would go on to be known as "Mr. and Mrs. Country Music."

His classic "Fire on the Strings" says it all and is hardly hyperbole as Joe Maphis blends individual pitches on virtually all tracks, including "Twin Banjo Special" and the prescient "Guitar Rock and Roll."

In 1955, Maphis moved up to parent label Columbia Records and cut his signature song, "Fire on the Strings." No truer words were ever written. The scorcher featured him playing banjo and mandolin along with his famous double-neck Mosrite electric guitar, made by Semie Moseley, with the upper neck tuned an octave higher. In 1957 he released his first LP, also titled *Fire on the Strings*, and in 1958 began performing and recording with 12-year old guitar protégé Larry Collins. The collaboration resulted in *Swingin' Strings*, which contained the spectacular "Hurricane." Maphis and Collins would perform on TV with Tex Ritter and Tennessee Ernie Ford many times, always to the delight and amazement of their fellow musicians and home audience. Maphis also played on Ricky Nelson's debut LP, in 1957, and he would become a regular guest on Jimmy Dean's TV show in the early 1960s. From 1961–63 Maphis recorded for Capitol Records, where he would cut *Country Music's Two Guitar Greats* with his old friend Merle Travis.

Maphis and his family moved to Nashville in 1968, and continued backing other artists and making his own until the 1980s. Along the way, he also helped discover Barbara Mandrell and was a mentor to Clarence White. On June 27, 1986, he succumbed to lung cancer, but his tremendous influence on country guitar lives on in the work of every hot country picker from Merle Travis to Danny Gatton to Brad Paisley.

How to Play It

"Flying Fingers" is a bopping boogie instrumental consisting of eighteen 6-measure choruses of A–D–A–E–A chord changes. Choruses 9–11 function as three improvised choruses and are "hot, hot, hot!" In measures 1–6 Maphis plays two guitar parts with Gtr. 1 on the standard-tuned lower neck of his double-neck Mosrite guitar, while Gtr. 2 carves out a complementary part on the upper neck, tuned an octave higher. Here everything is notated for regular standard-tuned guitar.

Gtr. 1 offers walking boogie woogie bass lines derived from the A, D, and E composite blues scales (1–2–♭3–3–4–♭5–5–6–♭7), respectively. In addition, Maphis throws in chromatic passing tones to connect the scale tones, as seen in measure 1 (Gtr. 1) and measures 1–2 (Gtr. 2), adding even more zip to the already insane lines. In measure 3, Maphis creates a distinct lead guitar part (Gtr. 2) separate from the rhythm guitar part (Gtr. 1).

In measures 7–12 and 13–18, Maphis drops the second guitar and flies solo with ripping, swinging, syncopated combinations of eighth and sixteenth notes that jump and jive like hillbillies on moonshine. He is so skillful at blending scales over the changes that his lines flow like they are powered by one long scale. This is especially evident in meas-ures 8–9, where the harmony shifts from A to D, and Maphis remains in fifth position, subtly adjusting his note selection to reflect the appropriate harmonic movement. Do not miss the funky unison licks in measure 10, where the open high E string is alternated with the fretted E note on string 2 at fret 5, to create musical tension and dynamic contrast against all the darting runs. Most closely identified with the blues and rock 'n' roll, this crafty move recalls such legendary guitarists as T-Bone Walker, Charlie Christian, and Chuck Berry.

Maphis connects choruses 2 and 3 (measures 12–13) with a run up the A composite blues scale, again blurring bar lines to add propulsion to his solo. He arrives at fret 5 and repeats the unison licks from measure 10, in measures 13–14. Maphis next reverses direction with a blistering descending run through measures 15–16, again nailing the changes, all the way down to a playful series of open low E notes, before lunging to the finish with a strong resolution to the tonic (A), in measure 18.

Vital Stats

Guitarist: Joe Maphis

Song: "Flying Fingers"

Album: *Fire on the Strings*, 1957

Age at time of recording: 36

Guitar: Custom Mosrite double-neck

Amp: Fender combo

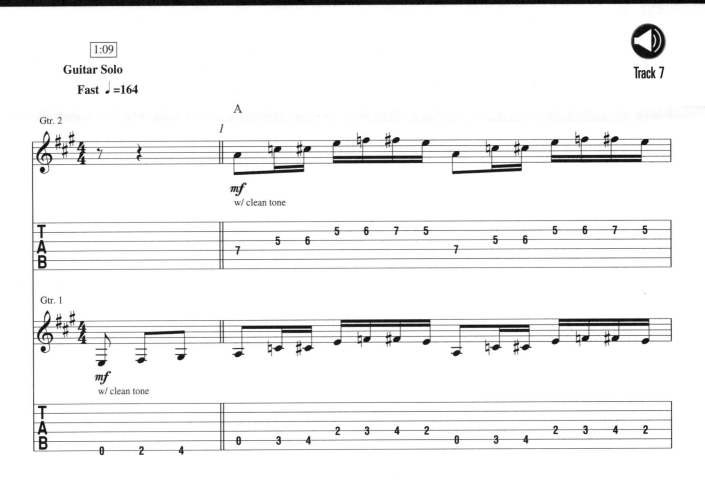

Flying Fingers

1:09

Guitar Solo

Fast ♩ =164

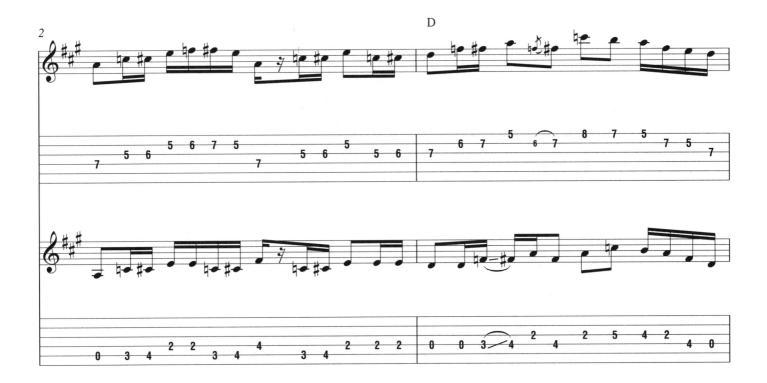

By Joe Maphis
© 1956 (Renewed) Vidor Publications, Inc.

Flying Fingers

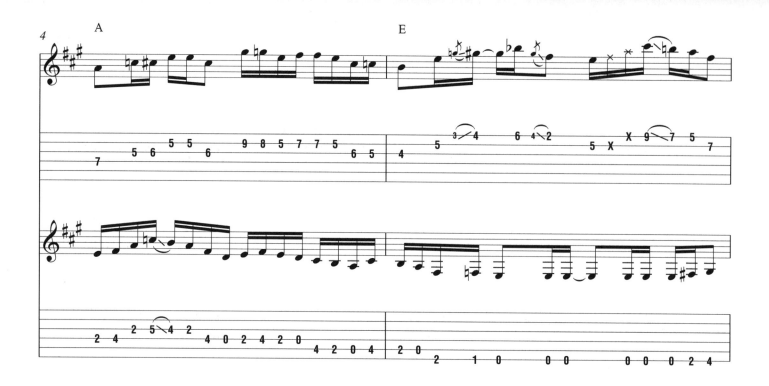

Gtr. 2 tacet

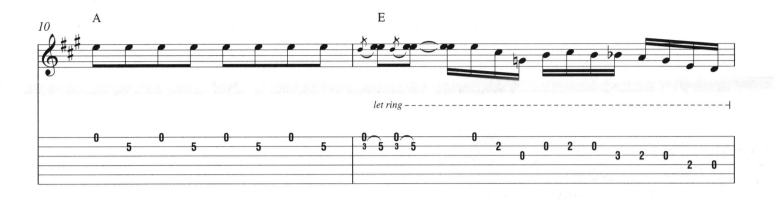

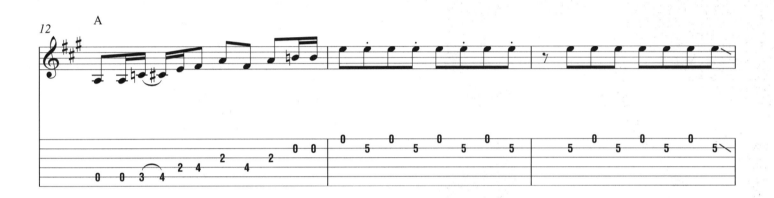

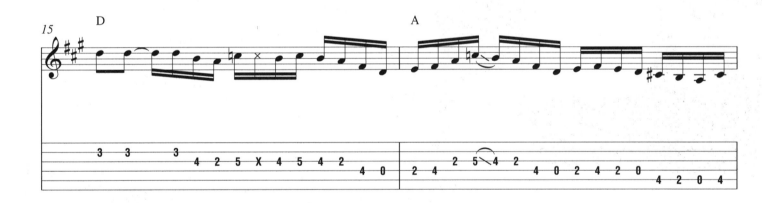

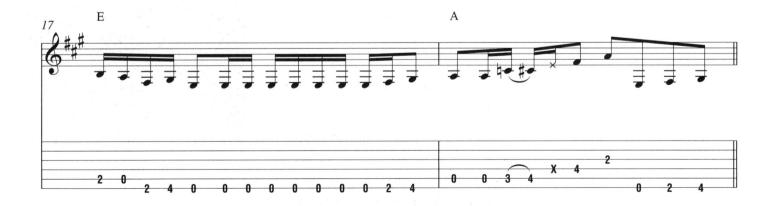

Luther Perkins

![Luther Perkins photo]

Courtesy R.A. Andreas/Cache Agency

"It was unorthodox, the way we worked it so that his guitar line matched my vocal."

—Johnny Cash on Perkins' guitar style

Johnny Cash, a.k.a. the "Man in Black," is a monumental presence in American music, with a long and storied career that spanned the early rumblings of rockabilly in the mid-1950s all the way through to his death at age 71, in 2003. A true original, his pioneering music received a significant boost from his first lead guitarist, Luther Perkins, who adapted Mother Maybelle Carter's style to create the famous Cash "boom chicka" sound.

Luther Monroe Perkins was born in Memphis, Tennessee on January 8, 1928, but grew up in Como, Mississippi. According to legend, as a kid he sold a load of old bricks to buy his first guitar, and he may have learned some guitar from Zeke Turner, Red Foley's guitarist. He returned to Memphis as a man and became a mechanic at the Auto Sales garage, working with fellow guitarists Marshall Grant and Roy Cash. When Cash's brother Johnny arrived in Memphis, in 1954, he, Grant, and Perkins began to pick guitars together. They formed a band around the singing and rhythm guitar of Cash. Grant, with no prior experience, bought an upright bass, while Perkins snared a beat-up Fender Esquire and a Sears Silvertone amp to play lead.

In September of 1954, they played their first pro gig, and by the end of the year they had a recording contract with Sam Phillips at Sun Records. "Cry Cry Cry"

b/w "Hey Porter" was the first single released in 1955, and Phillips named Perkins and Grant the "Tennessee Two," as the trio scored a spot on the famous radio show "Louisiana Hayride" for a year. "Folsom Prison Blues" arrived in 1956, followed by the #1 country hit "I Walk the Line," the lyrical content of which would prove quite ironic, given Cash's wild lifestyle. Tours were arranged, and the trio took to the road while *Johnny Cash and his Hot and Blue Guitar* (1957) became the first album released by Sun. Cash clashed with Phillips over royalties—as driven, headstrong artists are wont to do—however, and took his guys to Columbia, in 1958, where "Luther Played the Boogie" hit the country Top 10 in 1959 with his patented bass-string style. That same year, Cash became addicted to amphetamines, which would take a heavy toll on his health and demeanor. It also put a substantial strain on the band—especially Perkins, though he never complained and was even inwardly amused by some of his boss's hotel room antics. In 1960 drummer W.S. "Fluke" Holland, who previously played with rockabilly cat Carl Perkins (no relation to Luther), was added to make the

As minimal and iconic as all get out, Luther Perkins not only "walks the line" but the "Rock Island Line," as well as finding time to "Cry! Cry! Cry!" on his twangy bass strings.

group the "Tennessee Three." Luther Perkins would write a signature instrumental in the 1960s called "Bandana," which compared favorably with "Ghost Riders in the Sky," as a show opener for the band.

Cash finally got sober, in 1967, with help from his future wife June Carter, as well as from Perkins and Grant. A year later, the highlight of Perkins' career occurred when the band played at the notorious Folsom Prison, in California. A live recording was made showcasing Perkins' underrated and underappreciated skills, but unfortunately, it would be his last. On a tour of England in the spring of 1968, the heavy smoker came down with bronchitis, and Carl Perkins took over the lead guitar reins. Luther returned to the U.S. exhausted, even as Cash had a busy schedule ahead, including an appearance on the "Smothers Brothers Comedy Hour" and studio time booked to record *The Holy Land* album in Nashville.

On August 3, 1968, Perkins fell asleep in his house with a cigarette in his hand, causing a catastrophic fire that resulted in severe second and third degree burns. He never regained consciousness, and died two days later, on August 5. Cash was one of the pallbearers at his funeral and was reported to say, "Thank you, Luther," before the casket was lowered into the

ground. His heartfelt words could stand in for the thoughts and feelings of the entire country music community.

How to Play It

Like a lot of roots music from the 1950s, Luther Perkins' solo from "Folsom Prison Blues" looks deceptively simple. However, he follows the chord changes with unimpeachable logic, and on top of that employs cool inversions, to boot.

Perkins' twenty-two-measure solo, in the key of E, is essentially an elongated version of a 12-bar blues form, where each chord change gets double the normal measure count; for example, the I chord is initially played for eight bars, rather than four, as in the 12-bar form.

In measures 1–8, Perkins builds a hooky series of licks derived from the E composite blues scale (E–F#–G–G#–A–Bb–B–C#–D) in seventh position. This scale shape is based on the E major barre chord found at fret 7, as the second-inversion E major arpeggio in measure 8 confirms. This approach of envisioning chord shapes on the neck will provide quick entry into the world of country guitar soloing. To prove the

point, Perkins relocates to second position in measures 9–10 for a "long-form" A major fingering, with the pinky accessing the A note on string 1, at fret 5. Then, in measure 11 he moves up to fifth position for a first-inversion A major triad. Next, he scoots up four more frets to ninth position for a second-inversion A major shape, in measure 12. The effect is one of added IV-chord momentum and resultant tension.

Perkins drops back into rhythm-guitar mode in measures 13–22, as he "boom-chicka" strums on open-position E and B7 chord forms. Do not miss the classic country move in measure 20, where he pre-bends string 6 one-half step, from F# to G, strikes the note, releases it back to F#, and then resolves to the tonic, low E.

Vital Stats

Guitarist: Luther Perkins

Song: "Folsom Prison Blues"

Album: *Johnny Cash with His Hot and Blue Guitar*, 1957

Age at time of recording: 26

Guitar: Early 1950s Fender Esquire

Amp: Sears Silvertone 1300

Tune up 1/2 step:

(low to high) E#-A#-D#-G#-B#-E#

1:49

Guitar Solo

Moderate Country Two-step ♩ = 100

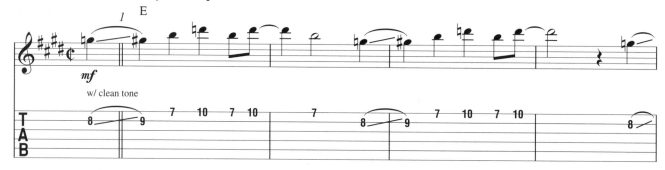

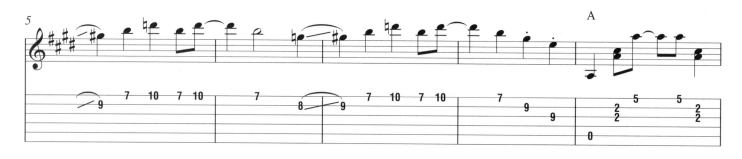

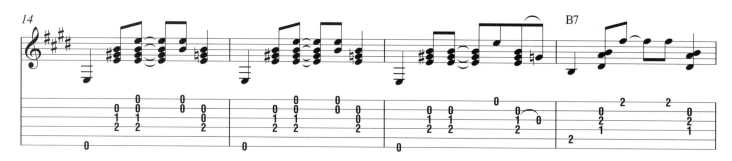

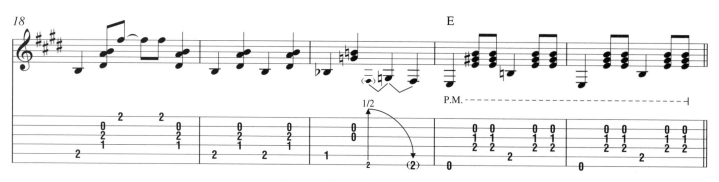

Words and Music by John R. Cash

James Burton

"I never bought a Ricky Nelson album, I bought a James Burton album."
—Keith Richards, introducing Burton at the Rock and Roll Hall of Fame

Courtesy of www.james-burton.net

Eric Hilliard Nelson, better known as "Ricky" and then "Rick," had every possible advantage on his way up the pop-rock ladder of success from 1957–1962, particularly his appearances on his family's hit TV show, "The Adventures of Ozzie and Harriet," which aired from 1952 until 1966. But give the teen idol his due: He was attracted to the hip rockabilly side of rock 'n' roll, and so enlisted first Joe Maphis, and then James Burton, to contribute smoking guitar licks to his records. Indeed, Nelson further helped inspire numerous guitarists by shining the spotlight on Burton at the end of each TV show.

James Burton was born in Dubberly, Louisiana, on August 21, 1939. Brought up in Shreveport, on the Gulf Coast, it was only natural that he would become one of the progenitors of swamp rock. The bedrock pioneering guitar music of Chet Atkins, Lightnin' Hopkins, Elmore James, Bo Diddley, and Chuck Berry reached his young ears through the radio, and by the age of 14, he was skipping school and playing clubs and parties. He

was so precocious that he was asked to join the staff band on the famous and influential "Louisiana Hayride." During his year in residency there, he learned to trade licks with pedal steeler Sonny Trammel in what would become a eureka moment for him, along with other up-and-coming country pickers.

By 1955, the 15-year old Burton was playing with proto-rocker Dale Hawkins and invented the classic, swampy guitar hook to "Susie-Q." When the restless Burton left Hawkins to work with rockabilly cat Bob Luman, he also was given the opportunity to go to Hollywood and appear in the movie *Carnival Rock*. More significantly, Ricky Nelson heard the band and invited Burton into his own backup band on his parents' TV show. Along with getting the spotlight in the closing musical segments, he also fully experienced the generosity and hospitality of the Nelsons, living with them for two years.

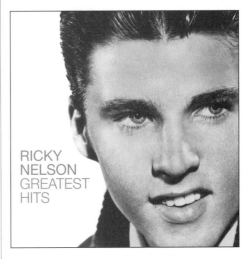

RICKY NELSON GREATEST HITS

James Burton literally made history and gave an impromptu guitar lesson every time he popped the strings to "pick the chicken," but also shows his sweeter, melodic side with "Never Be Anyone Else but You," "Travelin' Man," and "Fools Rush In."

Burton would continue to play with Nelson until 1967, while also finding time to be a member of the staff band on "Shindig!," in 1965. He also did sessions with Glen Campbell, the Everly Brothers, Dean Martin, Bobby Darin, and numerous others. Most important, though, was his work with Buck Owens and Merle Haggard in the late 1960s, helping to develop the "Bakersfield sound," which would come to have a huge influence on country and country rock music.

In 1969, Elvis Presley came calling, and Burton would remain with him until the aging idol's death, in 1977. Upon taking the Presley gig, Burton was honored with a signature paisley-finished Fender Telecaster. Later that year, he tracked his first solo album, called *Corn Pickin' and Slick Slidin'*, with steeler Ralph Mooney. He would also release *The Guitar Sounds of James Burton*, in 1971. In 1975, he powered Emmylou Harris's Hot Band for one year, before falling ill and turning the lead guitar chair over to one of the leading lights of the next generation of super-pickers, Albert Lee. When Presley died the following year, Burton was devastated, but he coped with the loss by throwing himself headlong into session work as well as working with John Denver for the next 15 years.

Refusing to stand still musically, Burton recorded the first of four albums with Elvis Costello, in 1986, and in 1987 he appeared prominently in a Cinemax special with Roy Orbison and friends, where he graciously suffered the ignominy of having to "trade fours" with an overeager and overmatched Bruce Springsteen. In the 1990s he suffered a severe accident at his home, but fortu-nately recovered and continued working with Denver. In 2001, Burton was inducted into the Rock and Roll Hall of Fame by Keith Richards, and in 2005 and 2007 he convened the first of his chari-table guitar festivals in Shreveport.

How to Play It

Burton picks it so smooth and sweet during his sixteen-measure solo that he sounds like he could be "back on the bayou" instead of in glitzy Hollywood. Of special note is his right-hand tech-nique: He holds a flatpick between his thumb and index finger in the usual fashion, but slips a fingerpick on his middle finger to access notes on the upper strings while concurrently picking bass notes. This approach is used exten-sively in measures 1–9, where he nails every root bass note with his flatpick at least once in each measure.

In measures 1–8, Burton explores basic open A, D7, and E7 chords, in a simple yet graceful and effective manner. For the A chord in measures 1, 2, 5, and 6, he barres the A major triad with his index finger at the second fret while accessing the A notes on string 1 with his pinky finger. Though the chord shapes are basic, Burton uses swing and syncopa-tion to make them compelling. The same holds true for the D7 voicings in meas-ures 3–4 and the E7 chords in measures 7–8, respectively. Notice the detail in measure 4, where Burton plays a B note on beat 3 that adds a bluesy 6th to the D chord but also leads to the oncoming A chord, in measure 5.

Burton maintains his open-position chord approach in measures 9–10 but then alters his thrust in measures 11–16, switching to scalar lines for the conclu-sion of the solo. Once again he makes the relatively simple sound compelling by using both the A major pentatonic (A–B–C#–E–F#) and A minor pentatonic (A–C–D–E–G) scale forms, in second and fifth positions, respectively, over the final six measures. In measures 11–12, drawing from the A major pentatonic scale, Burton makes sure to play the root of the underlying C# chord via a unison bend (whole step up from B), and then limits his note choices to F# (root) and A (b3rd), over the F#m chord.

Though likely pure intuition, Burton employs the gritty A minor pentatonic scale in measures 13 and 15, a move that is less definite as to the underlying harmony. Check out that neither measure 13 nor 14 (with a brief return to the A major penta-tonic) contains the root note of the under-lying chords. However, Burton does resolve the resulting tension by playing an A note on beat 1 of measures 15 and 16, completing one of the greatest and most imitated guitar solos of all time.

Vital Stats

Guitarist: James Burton

Song: "Hello Mary Lou"

Album: *Ricky Nelson Greatest Hits*, 2005

Age at time of recording: 22

Guitar: 1953 Fender Telecaster painted red

Amp: Fender Vibrasonic

Track 9

1:06

Guitar Solo

Moderately fast ♩ = 195

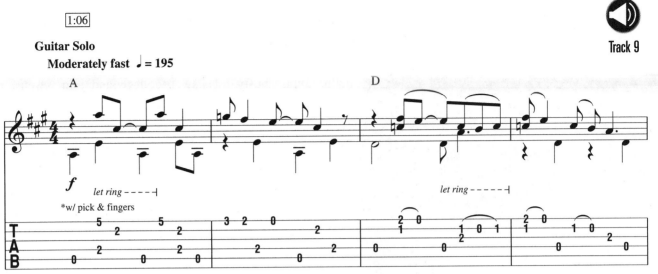

*w/ pick & fingers

*P.M. downstemmed notes throughout.

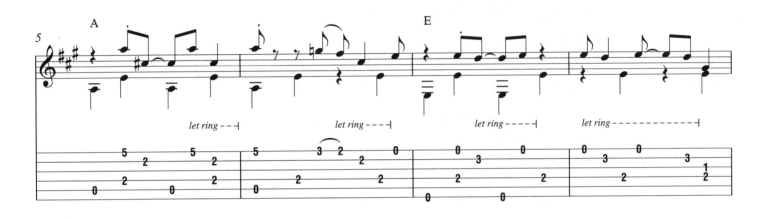

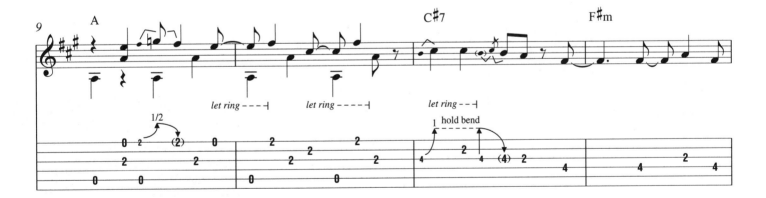

Don Rich

Photo provided by Michael Ochs Archives/Getty Images

*"The greatest
live chorus I
ever heard."*

**—Buck Owens referring to
Rich's playing on their cover
of "Johnny B. Goode"**

It would be a downright shame if all that Alvis Edgar "Buck" Owens was noted for was acting the hayseed and ogling the busty, Daisy Mae–type girls on "Hee Haw." Truth be told, the grinning fool with the tacky red, white, and blue guitars was one of the founding members of the honky-tonk "Bakersfield sound," along with Merle Haggard, Wynn Stewart, and Tommy Collins in northern California, in the 1960s. Owens also had been recommended to Columbia Records, albeit unsuccessfully, by none other than Joe Maphis, in the early 1950s. Indeed, he is often referred to as the first genuine country music star to boogie out of Bakersfield, and he enjoyed fifteen straight #1 hits in the 1960s. And right there at Owens' side through it all were the clean, snappy, and always tasty Telecaster licks of guitarist Don Rich.

Donald Eugene Ulrich was born on August 5, 1941, in Olympia, Washington. While in grade school, he took up the violin at his parents' urging, and later picked up the guitar as well. In 1959, while studying to be a music teacher, he met country musician Buck Owens, who had moved to Tacoma from Bakersfield in 1958 to become part-owner of a radio station, host a local TV show, and jump-start his performing career. Owens finally had his break-through hit (charting at #4) with "Under

Your Spell Again," featuring Rich on fiddle, and so in 1960 he returned to Bakersfield. Rich decided to leave college and join Owens, relocating to Bakersfield with his new wife. Touring with Owens made Rich want to play guitar, and Owens, wanting to concentrate on his vocals, gladly provided him the opportunity. In 1961, both men swapped their acoustic guitars for bright, twangy, maple-neck Fender Telecasters, though Owens would often call on Rich to saw away, with the disappointed response being, "Aw, chief!"

In 1963, Buck Owens and his Buckaroos, so-named by Merle Haggard when he played bass in the band, had their first of nineteen #1 hits in the 1960s with "Act Naturally," a catchy ditty covered a few years later by the Beatles. For Owens, who had been scuffling since the late 1940s, the tumultuous decade would prove to be a launching pad. In 1966 Owens was given a TV show called "Buck Owens' Ranch," and two years later he showed his crossover power by headlining at the Fillmore West. From 1969–71 he was the host for the national

Just in case you think Don Rich was merely a great "picker 'n' grinner" for country folk, check out what happens when he puts on his rock 'n' roll shoes for Chuck Berry's "Memphis."

production of "Hee Haw," with Rich and the Buckaroos in tow. That same year Rich recorded *The Buckaroos Play the Hits* with the band, as well as a solo titled *Fiddlin' Man*.

On July 17, 1974, following a session at the Buck Owens Studio, Rich hopped onto his motorcycle and left to join his family for a summer vacation. While riding near San Luis Obispo, California, he lost control of the bike, ran into a guardrail, and died, at age 32. Rich's tragic death precipitated a deep depression in Owens that lasted for years. Although his career was abbreviated, Rich's name is permanently engraved on the honored list of pioneering country guitarists.

How to Play It

Buck Owens had a #1 country single with "I've Got a Tiger by the Tail," thanks in part to Don Rich's economical, unfettered solo that proved the perfect complement to the chief's vocals. Like most postwar country guitarists, he uses the hybrid picking style that combines a flatpick with the bare middle finger. But that extra-sparkly tone, to go with the custom sparkle Tele that he got in 1966, is all his own invention.

The 16-measure progression is similar to the chorus (not shown), with a stop-time pickup measure from the preceding chorus. With a few exceptions, Rich follows standard country protocol by changing scales with the chords. Starting with a classic Tele sixth-string bend in the pickup measure, Rich stays on the "down-low" of the open-position E Mixolydian mode (E–F#–G#–A–B–C#–D) in measures on 1–2. In measures 3–4 he moves up a string-set to the A blues scale and leans exclusively on the A and G notes to define the A7 tonality. Maintaining this bright, bluesy sound, he slides up to the second-position B minor pentatonic scale in measures 5–6, for the B7 change. Closing out the first half of his solo, Rich drops back to the open-position bass register for measures 7–8. In measure 8, he also repeats that slick bend from the pickup measure, as a transition to the E chord in measure 9.

As opposed to his phrasing in measures 1–4, Rich starts in open position and then slides up to second position to nail the E–A tonality change across measures 9–12. Over A7, he alternates C# (3rd) and E (5th) notes, creating smooth forward momentum. Observe, too, the characteristic half-step bend and release of the fifth string, on beat 3 in measure 12, with resolution to the tonic open A. In measures 13–14, Rich hammers home the root, B, and gooses the momentum even more with a smooth, well-placed half-step slide midway through the bar. He then wraps it all up in a neat package with a tight, descending E Mixolydian line that not only ends the solo but also sets up the leisurely walk back up to the coming verse.

Vital Stats

Guitarist: Don Rich

Song: "I've Got a Tiger by the Tail"

Album: *I've Got a Tiger by the Tail* – Buck Owens and His Buckaroos, 1965

Age at time of recording: 24

Guitar: Early 1960s Fender Telecaster

Amp: Blackface Fender Twin Reverb

I've Got a Tiger by the Tail

Wayne Moss

Barefoot Jerry

—Wayne Moss's nickname

Whereas most latter-day "outlaw" country musicians connected to their rockabilly roots through a fondness for and familiarity with the genre's recordings, Waylon Jennings could claim true street cred. He not only was mentored by rockabilly pioneer Buddy Holly in the early 1950s but also played bass in the rockabilly pioneer's band on the ill-fated final tour, in 1959. Jennings mourned Holly's death for years, but would nevertheless go on to have a spectacular career from the 1970s on through the 1990s. Although Jennings was himself a decent guitarist, he let Wayne Moss, one of Nashville's finest, do the picking on the Jimmy Bryant–penned "The Only Daddy That Will Walk the Line."

With his experience in the "pop" side of country, Wayne Moss brings a sophisticated, melodic bent to the music apropos of his non-regulation issue Fender Jazzmaster on tunes like "Walk on Out of My Life" and the classic "Kentucky Woman."

Wayne Moss was born in Charleston, West Virginia, on February 9, 1938. He began playing guitar around the age of 8 with his mother's unconditional encouragement. By the time he was 15, he was a huge Chet Atkins fan, and his mother secured an interview with the country guitar legend to show off her offspring's skills. Atkins, less than impressed, was brutally candid and suggested Moss become a plumber instead.

Undeterred by his idol's assessment, Moss carried on. His experience in rock and R&B bands qualified him to become a member of Brenda Lee's backup band in the early 1960s. He then joined Charlie McCoy and the Escorts—the hottest band in Nashville in the 1960s—featuring future country stars Charlie McCoy on harmonica and various other instruments (sometimes played all at once), and Kenny Buttrey on drums. Moss started Cinderella Studios in 1962 and also worked at RCA with his old "mentor," Chet Atkins. Through the years Moss would play with a wide range of artists, including Patsy Cline, Ray Price, Slim Whitman, the Monkees, Dolly Parton, Roy Orbison (he played the signature riff on "Pretty Woman"), Buffy Sainte-Marie, Jerry Jeff Walker, Al Kooper, Steve Miller, Willie Nelson, Leo Kottke, Kris Kristofferson, and Peter, Paul & Mary.

In 1966, some of Nashville's top session musicians, including Moss and McCoy,

Courtesy R.A. Andreas/Cache Agency

played on Bob Dylan's monumental *Blonde on Blonde* double album. Moss recalls that, at one point in the session, the bard asked for some time away from recording so he could change a few words on the eleven-minute track "Sad-Eyed Lady of the Lowlands"—a break that lasted into the next day. So when Moss and company were called to record *Nashville Skyline*, in 1969, and Dylan made the same request for another song, Moss went into a corner with a nylon string guitar and began writing his own song, only to have the offended Dylan fire him on the spot.

That same year, following the Dylan album, the group from the session formed Area Code 615 with Moss, Buttrey, McCoy, guitarists Mac Gayden and Bobby Thompson, pedal steeler Weldon Myrick, keyboardists David Briggs and Ken Lauber, bassist Norbert Putnam and fiddler Buddy Spicher. The instrumental combo could be seen as Nashville's answer to Booker T & the MGs, who hailed from Memphis. Following their debut, *Area Code 615*, which included contemporary covers like "Hey Jude," they recorded *Trip to the Country* (1970). The album contained "Stone Fox Chase," which became the theme song for the lauded BBC music program "The Old Grey Whistle Test." Despite critical praise and hippie cult status, they disbanded after playing only one engagement, at the Fillmore West in 1970, due to the members' various other musical commitments. McCoy would become musical director for "Hee Haw," while Moss went on to form the late, lamented country-rocking Barefoot Jerry in 1971, with Gayden, Buttrey, and keyboard player John Harris. Despite many personnel changes and some label hopping, the group lasted until 1977. Recently, a rare live album was released (www.barefootjerry.com). After their demise, Moss went back to doing sessions and running his Cinderella Studio, the oldest continuously running recording studio in the Nashville area.

How to Play It

The twenty-one-measure solo, despite its pedestrian I–IV–V–I (E–A–B7–E) changes, is an unusual arrangement for country music. This is made especially evident with the bar of 2/4 time tossed in at measure 17, which is the final bar of the stop-time section that echoes Jennings' vocal verses.

In measures 1–4, Moss employs the E Mixolydian mode (E–F♯–G–A–B–C♯–D) as the foundation for his plucky chicken-pickin' lines. Here, the percussive eighth-note triplets are, in essence, just muted B notes (fret 7, string 1). To sound these, simply release just enough fret-hand pressure to mute the note. He follows the chicken pickin' immediately with the first of several pedal steel–style bends—a half-step pre-bend and release move—littered throughout the solo. In measure 3, Moss uses another classic pedal steel–type bend, an *oblique* bend, to create a B/G♯ (5th/3rd) double stop that conclusively nails down the E major tonality. Execute this bend with your ring finger, while holding down the stationary B note with your pinky finger.

In measures 5–8, Moss climbs up to the tenth-position A Mixolydian (A–B–C♯–D–E–F♯–G) scale shape, culminating in the F♯ note at fret 14 on string 1, to bridge the A–B7 change in measures 8–9. This move places Moss comfortably in twelfth position and the B Mixolydian mode (B–C♯–D♯–E–F♯–G♯–A). Starting in measure 12 and continuing in measure 13, Moss shifts to another soloing concept, bending G♯ up a half step to A, where it functions as a ♭7th in search of resolution. The propulsive repetition further contributes to the dynamic musical tension, before Moss offers some relief in the form of a repeated whole-step bend from C♯ to D♯ (3rd), followed by resolution to B, to end the phrase.

Moss next tumbles down the fingerboard like a speckled pup chasing a ball. For the stop-time phrase in measures 15–17, he starts with a consonant E whole note, before a minor 2nd–inflected phrase leads to two oblique bends in a measure of 2/4. Moss saves his best pedal steel licks for the final four bars, rolling some of the sweetest sounds this side of Jerry Donahue off his fingers. He kicks off the festivities with yet another oblique bend (G♯/E double stop), and then skips nimbly down the E composite blues scale (E–F♯–G–G♯–A–B♭–B–C♯–D) before concluding with an open, low E thump.

Vital Stats

Guitarist: Wayne Moss

Song: "The Only Daddy That Will Walk the Line"

Album: *Only the Greatest –* Waylon Jennings, 1968

Age at time of recording: 30

Guitar: Pre-CBS Fender Jazzmaster

Amp: Ampeg combo

Track 11

Tune down 1/2 step:
(low to high) Eb-Ab-Db-Gb-Bb-Eb

1:06

Guitar Solo

Moderately ♩ = 161

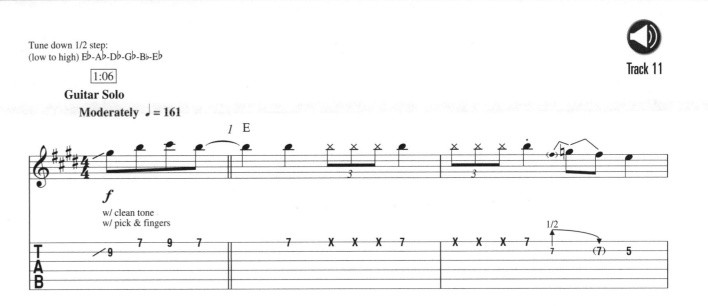

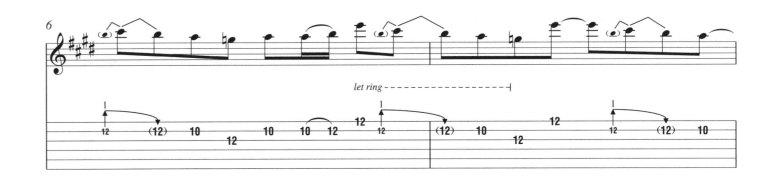

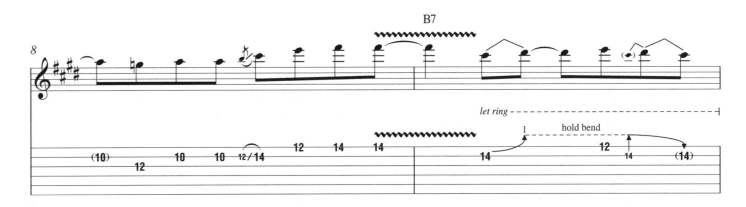

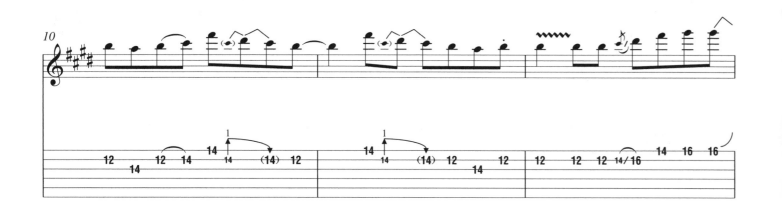

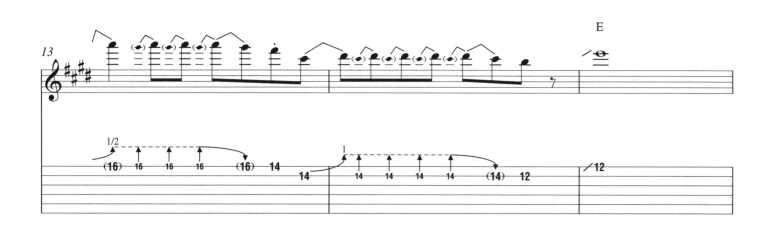

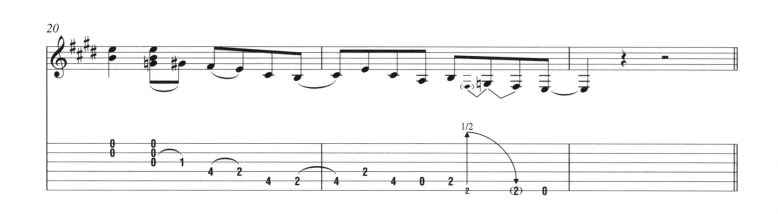

Roy Nichols

"...sounds like horsey fartin'..."

—Rose Maddox describing Nichols' playing on the bass strings

Merle Haggard's redneck rant "Okie from Muskogee," in 1969, led to a request for him to endorse presidential candidate George Wallace. Haggard refused, and he later declined to play it for President Richard Nixon at the White House as well. Unfortunately, the controversial tune deflected attention from the substantial contribution that Haggard made to the evolution of country music in the 1960s. The "real deal," he lived the life often romanticized in country songs; for instance, he actually served time in prison, though he was officially pardoned in 1972 by then California governor Ronald Reagan. In 1974, he played on Western swing legend Bob Wills' final album, *For the Last Time*, and was bequeathed Wills' fiddle upon his death a year later. Additionally, Haggard helped create the Bakersfield honky tonk sound, and always had slick pickers like James Burton, Roy Nichols, and later, Redd Volkaert, in his band. Nichols, who brought a wild unpredictability fueled by his devastating technique, was Haggard's man when he recorded "Honky Tonk Night Time Man," in 1974.

Roy Ernest Nichols was born in Chandler, Arizona, on October 21, 1932, to Bruce and Lucille, who moved the family to Fresno, California, in 1934. Bruce played upright doghouse bass and taught 11-year old Roy to play three chords on the guitar, so he could accompany his father at local dances. Legend has it that Roy first became interested in playing when he overheard Gypsies performing at night around a campfire just outside his parents' property. By age 14, the younger Nichols was good enough to play for pay on the weekends, and at 16 he went on the road playing seven nights a week and reportedly recording 100 songs with the popular Maddox Brothers and Rose. Before he was 18, Nichols was playing regularly on a morning radio show in Hanford, California. In the early 1950s, he spent a few years touring and recording with country star Lefty Frizzell. Heavily influenced by Gypsy jazz legend Django Reinhardt and seemingly never at a loss for work due to his prodigious talent, Nichols played the clubs while also touring and recording with Johnny Cash, Buck Owens, Faron Young, Cliffie Stone, and others. From 1955–59 Nichols scored another daily live radio gig with Cousin Herb Hensen's Radio Post Gang country music show in Bakersfield, the hotbed of the emerging honky-tonk sound that would rescue country music from the overproduced, syrupy mash that was coming out of Nashville.

A move to Las Vegas, Nevada, in 1960, would prove providential as he worked and recorded with Wynn Stewart at the Nashville Nevada Club. In 1962, Haggard (on bass) joined the band that also included Glen Campbell and pedal steeler Ralph Mooney, and in 1963 they

Courtesy of www.shownet.com.au

recorded four tracks. By 1965 Nichols and his young family were back in Bakersfield, and when Haggard left Stewart to form the Strangers in late 1965, Nichols was his first hire. Before long Merle Haggard & the Strangers were no strangers on the country charts, as Nichols displayed his characteristic

MERLE HAGGARD AND THE STRANGERS

Presents His 30th Album
A Working Man Can't Get Nowhere Today

Like all the best country pickers, Roy Nichols knew the blues and makes it his own on the ironic "White Man Singin' the Blues," as well as "Moanin' the Blues" and "Blues for Dixie."

pre-bends and "chicken pickin'" to great effect.

The fleet-fingered Tele-master would remain with Haggard until 1987, at which time he retired from playing professionally. In 1988 he was inducted into the Western Swing Society Hall of Fame in Sacramento. Tragically, in 1996 he suffered a stroke that left him partially paralyzed and unable to play. A man with an indomitable spirit, however, his response was to say, "I can't physically play the guitar anymore, but I still play it mentally everyday." On July 3, 2001, he died, fittingly, in Bakersfield, where he had helped foment a musical revolution over thirty years earlier.

How to Play It

Roy Nichols says more in a single 12-bar chorus of "Honky Tonk Night Time Man" (originally released on *Merle Haggard Presents his 30th Album*, in 1974) than many contemporary country guitarists could in several extended choruses of the same form. Of course, the fact that nearly the entire solo comprises sixteenth-note phrases, whereas other mere mortals would play relatively sedate eighth notes, further intensifies the impression that his

solo is jam-packed with action. Using the G composite blues scale (G–A–B♭–B–C–D♭–D–E–F) combined with the G major pentatonic scale (G–A–B–D–E), as well as a boat load of chromatic passing tones, Nichols crafts a ride as exciting as moonshiners barreling down a gravel road while being pursued by the law.

As opposed to most of his contemporaries who change scales with each chord change, Nichols focuses his interest on a relatively confined group of notes in third position. Consequently, his negotiating of the G, C, and D chords is subtle, though decisive, and contributes to the rollicking nature of the solo. He kicks off the adventure with a repetitive motif up the G major pentatonic scale, starting on the 3rd (B). For the next three measures, Nichols snaps off strings of skittery notes, all the while highlighting the chord tones G, B, and D. When the harmony shifts to the IV chord, C, in measures 5–6, Nichols makes sure to shift the emphasis to the C, E, and G chord tones. Observe that these notes are all contained in the G composite blues scale, thus making them readily accessible to his dancing fingers. Nichols turns his attention back to the G chord in measures 7–8, with bluesy, descending lines and a classic unison bend from C to D, which he sustains across the bar line, providing a dynamic change from the preceding rapid-fire phrases.

The solo shifts to the V chord (D) in measure 9, and Nichols pulls out a variation on the G major pentatonic motif that opened the solo. This move serves as a compositional motif to help tie the solo together. In measure 10, he cleverly bangs on a C note, which functions as the ♭7th to draw the ear into the oncoming chord change. With great skill Nichols navigates up to the scale's top strings, emphasizing the D (5th) and G (root) chord tones in measure 11, and then ends his wild and zany excursion through the basic country changes conclusively with the G note on beat 3 of measure 12. Be aware that, unlike most 12-bar progressions, this one concludes with the I (G) chord, rather than the V (D), to create an easy transition back into the vocal verse.

Vital Stats

Guitarist: Roy Nichols

Song: "Honky Tonk Night Time Man"

Album: *Merle Haggard Presents His 30th Album*, 1974

Age at time of recording: 42

Guitar: Fender Telecaster

Guitar Solo
Moderately fast ♩ = 135

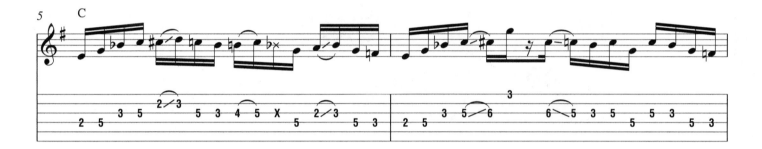

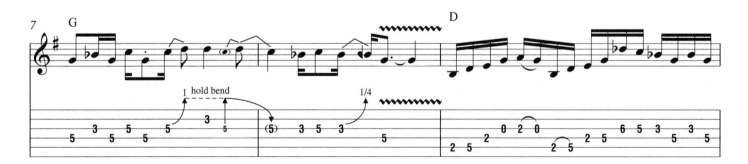

Jerry Reed

Photo by Doug McKenzie/Getty Images

A virtuoso guitarist, prolific songwriter, slick session man, and ingratiating movie actor, country music icon Jerry Reed has had a spectacular career. From the 1950s rockabilly era to the counterculture 1960s to the pop Nashville sounds of the 1970s and 1980s, his versatility has afforded him bountiful opportunities to display his many talents. Reed considers himself an entertainer, but there is good

"I was toppin' cotton, son."

—Jerry Reed on his recording sessions with Elvis

reason that he is known first and foremost as the "Guitar Man."

Jerry Reed Hubbard was born to Robert and Cynthia Hubbard on March 20, 1937, in Palmetto, Georgia. His mother sang gospel music and played guitar, buying her young son a $7 acoustic and teaching him his first chords. He initially used nickels for picks before discovering the thumbpick and the pioneering fingerstyle technique of the immortal Merle Travis. When, at his one and only guitar lesson, he was strongly advised to lose the thumbpick in exchange for a flatpick, he high-tailed it out and never looked back.

In 1955, while living in Atlanta, the 17-year old Reed signed with Capitol Records, for whom he would record ten

country and rock 'n' roll singles. Rockabilly heartthrob Gene Vincent would cover one of those songs, "Crazy Legs," in 1958. In 1960, Reed's "That's All You Gotta Do" became a #5 hit for Brenda Lee as the flipside of her #1 charter, "I'm Sorry." After leaving Capitol and completing his Army service, Reed moved his family to Nashville, in 1961, to do session work for Columbia Records. In 1964, he sought his release from the label for the express purpose of latching on with his idol, Chet Atkins, at RCA Records. The two became fast friends, and Atkins produced Reed's first chart hit with "Guitar Man," in 1967. Atkins always said that Reed, with his five-finger right-hand technique called "the claw" (which was also the title of his 1967 signature instrumental), was the better fingerpicker, and in fact had helped him arrange his famous "Yakety Axe."

In 1970, Reed crossed over to the pop audience with the swamp-rocking "Amos Moses," shared a GRAMMY® with Atkins for *Me and Jerry*, and then followed with the prophetic "When

Jerry Reed may have deferred to heartthrob Burt Reynolds onscreen, but his jubilant picking put him front and center among the giants of country guitar.

You're Hot You're Hot," which went to #8 in 1971, becoming his top seller and helping him garner a GRAMMY® Award for Best Male Country Performance. In addition he became a regular on Glen Campbell's TV show.

The leap from television to the movies was a short one for the charismatic "good ol' boy." Starting in 1974 he co-starred with his running buddy Burt Reynolds in a string of movies, including all three of the pop-culture classic *Smokey and the Bandit* films. The soundtrack to the first one, in 1977, produced a #2 hit for Reed in "East Bound and Down."

After having put his music career on the back burner for a spell, Reed picked up his guitar again in earnest and won another GRAMMY®, in 1992, for Best Country Instrumental Performance, for "Sneakin' Around," with Atkins. A comedy/music album *Flyin' High* was released in 1995, and he appeared with Adam Sandler in *The Waterboy* in 1998. That same year he recorded *Old Dogs* with Waylon Jennings, Mel Tillis, and Bobby Bare. In 2005 he released the aptly titled *Jerry Reed: Live Still!* And in 2006 he put out *Let's Git It On*, an album that reveals his fret-punishing and swampy songwriting skills, along with his ribald humor, to be fully intact.

On August 30, 2008, Reed died at the age of 71 from complications resulting from emphysema. He remained active up to the end, virtually writing his own epitaph with, "There'll be no retirement for this cowboy. I want to work hard and play hard all the days of my life." Both his singing and guitar voices will be missed.

How to Play It

Jerry Reed has "big ears," literally and figuratively, and apparently became enamored with the mercurial flatpicking of jazz wizard George Benson in the 1970s. Consequently, in this solo he flatpicks, using only his thumbpick, which is perfectly in keeping with the crisply picked, single-note lead lines in attendance.

Reed's solo in "East Bound and Down" is twenty-four measures long and played over an ABA arrangement. Each A section comprises G–A7–F–C–D–G–A7–F–D–G changes, while the B section uses a Em–C–A7–B7–Em–B7–Em–C–A7–B7 progression. Understand that the G–A7 (I–II) chord change in the A section is often used in country music to create a feeling of "uplift."

Check out how Reed plays the melody with Gtr. 2, but overdubs Gtr. 1 throughout for harmony and unison lines that serve to both sweeten and fatten up his sound. With few exceptions, Reed employs the open-position G major pentatonic scale (G–A–B–D–E), colloquially called the "Nashville scale" by country pickers. If you're not familiar with major pentatonic fingerings, you can also envision the scale as the open-position E *minor* pentatonic scale, only you resolve to G, not E.

Throughout the solo, Reed bases his improvisation on the vocal melody, resulting in an easily hummable solo. In fact, Gtr. 1 essentially functions as the backing vocal on the track. And just as vocal lines are derived from the harmony, so too does Reed follow suit

with his embellishments. For instance, in the guitar fill that is measure 4, he switches to the D composite blues scale (D–E–F–F#–G–Ab–A–B–C), to provide some bluesy interplay between the b3rd (F) and major 3rd (F#).

In the B section, which is cast in the darker tonality of the relative minor key, Reed keeps the diesel truckin' with a galloping rhythmic motif applied to the E minor scale (E–F#–G–A–B–C–D), in measures 9–10 and 13–14. Using a flatpick facilitates the brisk alternate picking necessary for efficient execution of this rhythm. Taking artistic liberties in measures 15, Reed applies a dynamic downshift to eighth notes and quarter notes, before finishing with a nimble run up the fingerboard to bring his solo back home to the A section.

To close out the solo, Reed repeats measures 1–8, further driving home the song's vocal melody. Perhaps because it was for a movie soundtrack, Reed played rather conservatively. Nevertheless, his fat, smooth, overdriven tone and rich harmony lines deliver a satisfying repast for the ears.

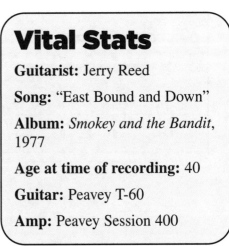

Vital Stats

Guitarist: Jerry Reed

Song: "East Bound and Down"

Album: *Smokey and the Bandit*, 1977

Age at time of recording: 40

Guitar: Peavey T-60

Amp: Peavey Session 400

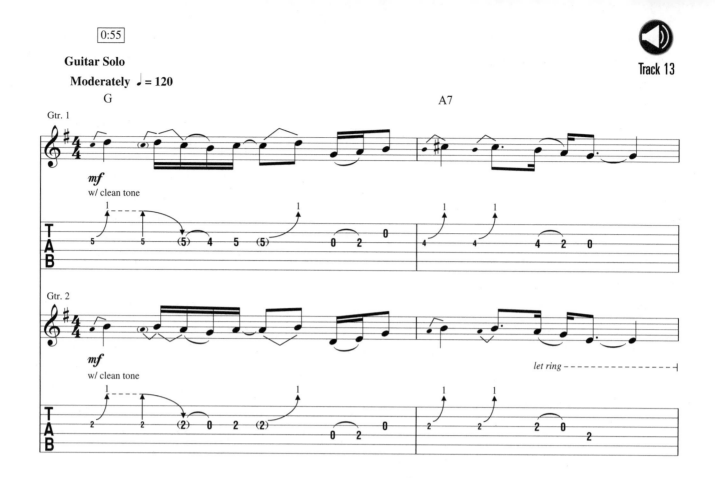

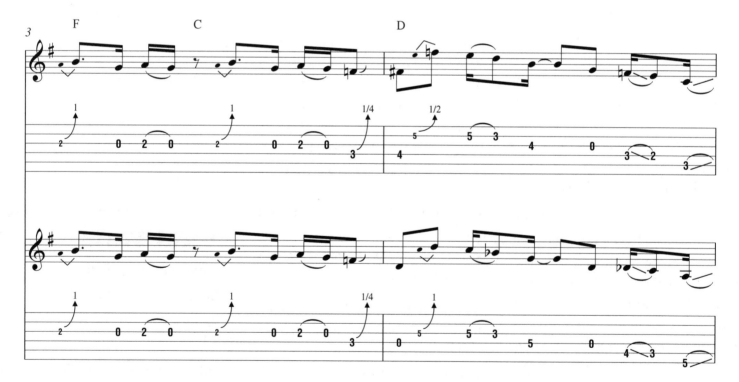

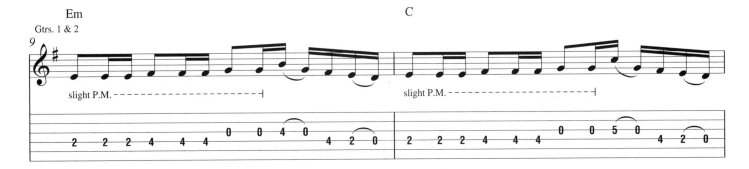

East Bound and Down

Albert Lee

Photo © Peter Mazel/Sunshine/Retna Ltd.

> *"...the solo on the live version of 'Cocaine' is so un-Eric-like."*

—Albert Lee referring to his solo from Clapton's live album *Just One Night*

There is something about postwar British musicians, especially guitarists, that allows them to tap into American roots music and reproduce it with great fidelity and expressiveness. Whatever that something is, Albert Lee has it in spades, winning *Guitar Player* magazine's Best Country Guitarist award five times. On the strength of his breathtaking chops, he has been not only one of country guitar's top guns but a downright certifiable modern guitar hero.

Lee was born in Herefordshire, England, on December 21, 1943. His father played piano and accordion, and young Albert began learning the classics and pop tunes on the piano at the age of 7. The birth of rock 'n' roll in 1950s Memphis, however, stoked in him a love for Jerry Lee Lewis and rockabilly music. Lee began playing the guitar around 1958, and a newfound interest in Buddy Holly soon expanded to include a fascination with country guitar, as he absorbed the music of the Louvin Brothers, Jimmy Bryant, Cliff Gallup with Gene Vincent, and James Burton with Ricky Nelson. Nashville session ace Hank Garland's crossover classic *Jazz Winds from a New Direction* (1960) was another ear- and eye-opener.

After quitting school at age 16 and subsequently enduring a series of day gigs, Lee decided he was not cut out for the straight life and joined an R&B cover band in 1961. A year later he cut his first record with the Jury. As was a rite of passage for British rock bands in the early 1960s, grueling tours in Germany with the Nightsounds followed, as Lee ground out the rock hits of Jerry Lee Lewis, Chuck Berry, Eddie Cochran, and Little Richard day and night. Back in London he encountered a developing club scene rife with future guitar slingers. Lee replaced Jimmy Page in Mike Hurst's band and in the Crusaders, only to have Ritchie Blackmore take his place when he joined Chris Farlowe and the Thunderbirds in 1964. Farlowe had gravitated from rock to R&B and led one of the more established bands in London, scoring a contract with Andrew Loog Oldham's Immediate label in 1966. Lee left the following year and played around, ending up in the progressive country rock group Cabin Fever for eighteen months. Tired of the hostile reception they received from conservative English fans, Lee split and closed out the decade doing session work.

In 1970, Poet & the One Man Band morphed into Heads, Hands & Feet, as Lee replaced Jerry Donahue, and the legendary country-fueled band of British rock veterans signed for the largest advance to date. They stayed together until 1972, producing three albums that showcased Lee's guitar as well as his piano playing and vocals to a degree. Their self-titled debut, in 1971, contained the first version of Lee's stunning signature song, "Country Boy."

Lee would get the chance to play and record with Buddy Holly's Crickets before settling in Los Angeles and its highly competitive session scene. He backed Joe Cocker in 1974, and the following year he began working on a solo album, but it lay in the can until 1978, when he redid most of the tracks.

Albert Lee does not feel the need to test the metallurgy of his strings on every single track, but does provide exemplary and exhilarating fret work throughout, as heard on "Setting Me Up," "Rock 'n' Roll Man," and "Real Wild Child (Wild One)."

Meanwhile, he joined Emmylou Harris's Hot Band in 1976, replacing his idol James Burton, who was still committed to backing Elvis. Lee left the Hot Band in 1978 to pursue a solo career and finish *Hiding*, an album on which he not only played guitar, keyboards, and mandolin, but also sang. A trip back to London for Christmas resulted in Lee meeting Eric Clapton, with whom he played and recorded for the next five years. By all accounts, Lee often had to push the notoriously lazy Slowhand into playing up to his potential. In 1983, after Clapton cleaned house and assembled a brand new band, Lee was responsible for reuniting the feuding Everly Brothers and played on and off with them for many years.

Lee then released the instrumental albums *Speechless* (1987) and *Gagged But Not Bound* (1988). However, in 1987 Gerry Hogan had inveigled him to lead his band Hogan's Heroes—a position he still holds. An endorsement with Ernie Ball led to a turn with their sponsored Biff Baby All-Stars, featuring Eddie Van Halen, Steve Lukather, and Steve Morse. In 1996 he recorded with Bill Wyman's Rhythm Kings and also toured with the ex-Stones bassist and his band.

Lee is known in the industry as a generous musician, one who checks his ego at the door. And even now, with his career in its fifth decade, he continues to spread his unabated love of country guitar. In 2002 he received a GRAMMY® for Best Country Instrumental Performance, for "Foggy Mountain Breakdown," from *Earl Scruggs and Friends*. Maintaining his solo career, he recorded *Heartbreak Hotel* followed by *Road Runner* in 2006.

How to Play It

Guaranteed to bring the house down whenever he plays it, "Country Boy" is proof positive of Albert Lee's awesome chops. And if there is any irony in this proud son of Britannia singing, "I may look like a city slicker, shinin' up through my shoes, underneath I'm just a cotton picker, pickin' out a mess of blues," it is lost on his audiences, most of who came to see Lee's shiny fretwork.

Front and center in Lee's eighty-two-measure outro solo is his crafty use of the delay effect, which creates the air of nonstop super-fast chicken pickin'. To create this sound, Lee sets his delay pedal to repeat his quarter notes one and a half beats later, so that his runs become thrilling eighth-note romps. Here's how you can do it. First, divide 60 by the song's tempo (quarter note = 300 bpm): 60/300 = 0.200. Next, because you want the repeated note to occur one and a half beats later, you multiply 0.200 by 1.5, which equals 0.300. Now, remove the decimal point, and this number becomes your delay setting in milliseconds: 300 ms. Then, set your feedback, or regeneration, knob to 0, to produce only one repeat, and set your effect level to 100 percent, so each delay-produced note sounds equal in volume to the picked notes. The real trick to using this technique, though, is training your internal feedback loop (ear to brain to picking hand) to play in quarter notes while hearing in eighth notes. It's tricky at first, but once you get it, it's quite easy.

The structure may be seen as a repeating ten-measure sequence of E–A7–D7–G chord changes, with the final four measures of each sequence being a stop-time "chorus" over G. The exception is in measures 71–82, where the progression is twelve measures long, with E–A7–C–D changes culminating with four measures of stop-time in E. It is particularly important to be aware of the chord changes in this solo, because Lee matches his scales to the chords, as opposed to most blues and rock guitarists, who use the key-center soloing approach.

Observe that in measures 1–26 and 51–74, the E–A7–D7 changes are delineated with boogie bass lines derived from each chord's diatonic scale. Rather than repeat the typically ascending lines each go-round as a bassist might do, Lee keeps it fresh by playing descending lines in measures 4, 6, and 22, and with chromatic lines in measures 24–25. Not to be discounted is his tendency to play some walking-type lines on the top strings, especially for the D7 changes in measures 6–7, and in 25–26.

Lee shifts smoothly to the G composite blues scale (G–A–Bb–B–C–Db–D–E–F) for his stop-time runs. The ascending series of 3rds in measures 27–30 not only adds a vibrant layer of harmony to the proceedings but also provides a relentless transition to the twelfth position, where he plays measures 31–36. Lee caps it all off in measures 79–82 with a descending 3rds sequence that cascades like cool country water down a mountain stream.

Vital Stats

Guitarist: Albert Lee

Song: "Country Boy"

Album: *Hiding*, 1979

Age at time of recording: 36

Guitar: 1953 Fender Telecaster

Amp: Music Man combo

2:30

Guitar Solo

Fast Two-beat ♩ = 150

f

w/ clean tone & delay

slight P.M. throughout

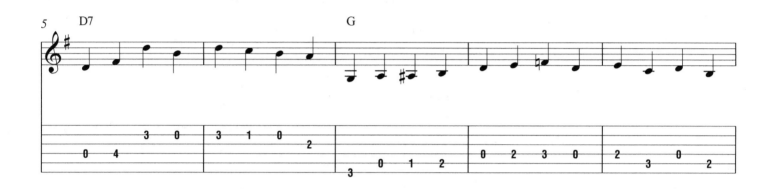

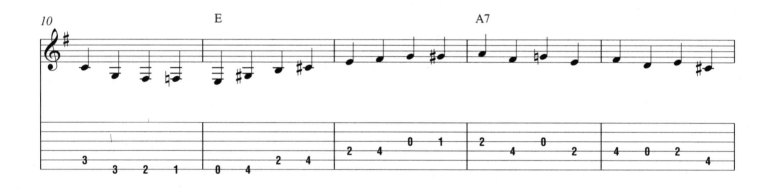

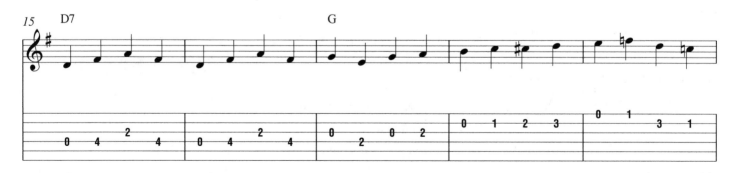

Words and Music by Tony Colton, Ray Smith and Albert Lee
Copyright © 1971 JAMARNIE MUSIC
Copyright Renewed
All Rights for the United States and Canada Controlled and Administered by UNIVERSAL - POLYGRAM INTERNATIONAL PUBLISHING, INC.
All Rights Reserved   Used by Permission

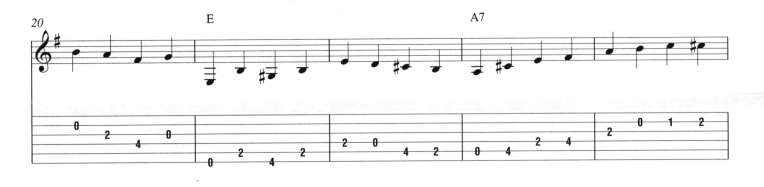

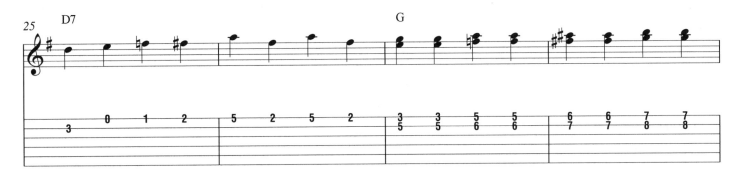

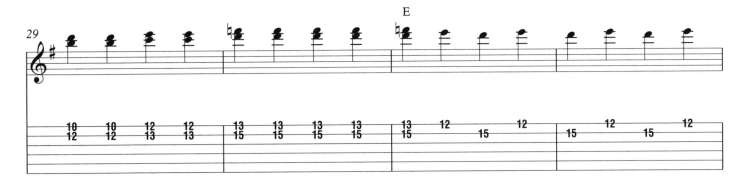

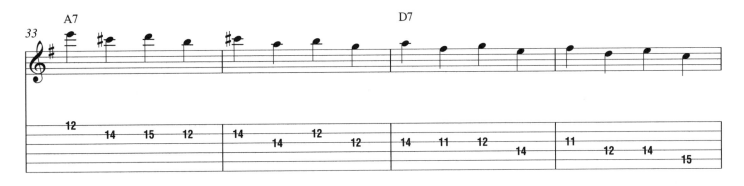

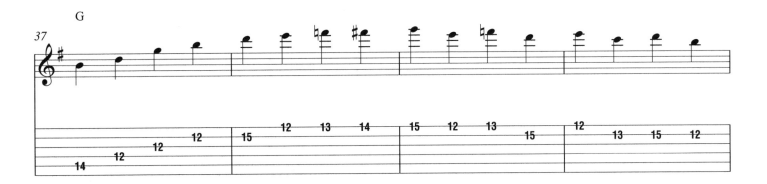

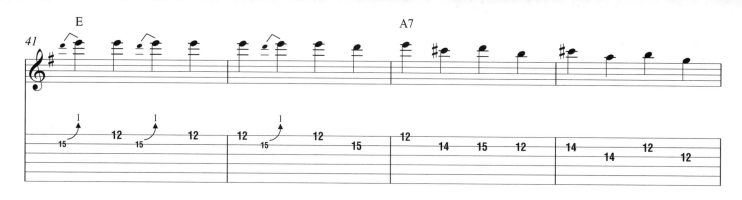

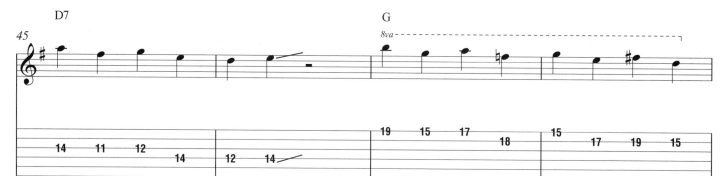

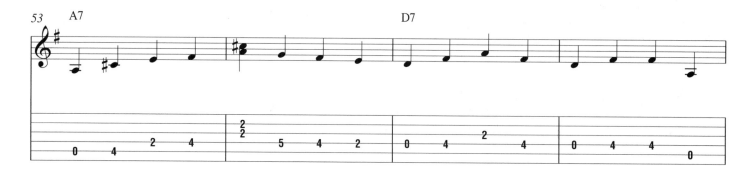

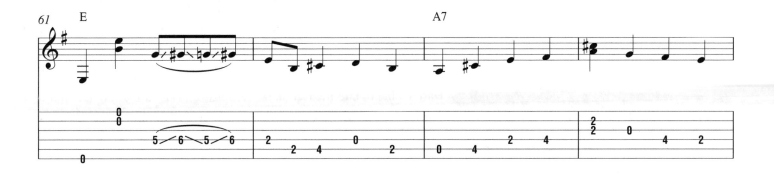

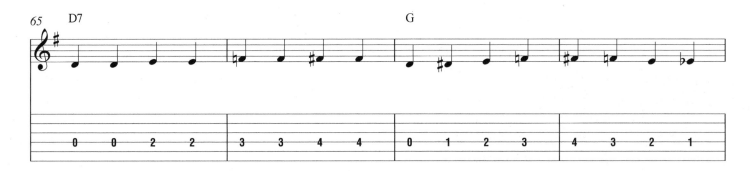

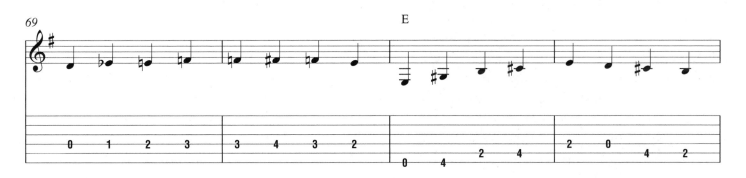

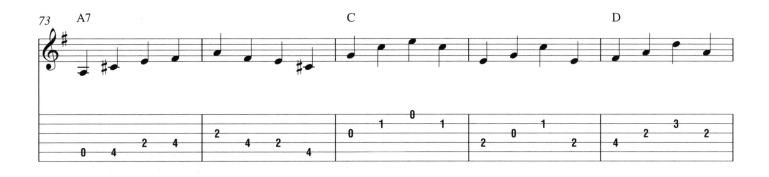

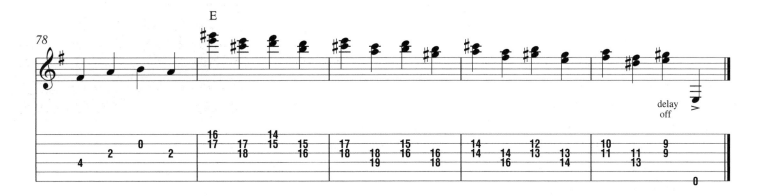

Ray Flacke

> ## *"The phrase 'super picker' applies to Ray Flacke."*
>
> —Carl Perkins

Singer and multi-instrumentalist Ricky Skaggs was a young phenom in the early 1960s, making an appearance on TV with Flatt & Scruggs when he was just 7 years old. At the age of 15 he was playing in bluegrass legend Ralph Stanley's band, where he further honed his fast and clean flatpicking chops. In 1977, he would follow Rodney Crowell as guitarist in Emmylou Harris's band, and then in late 1982, Skaggs became the youngest member of the Grand Ole Opry. He would next have an amazing run of five straight #1 country singles from 1982 until 1983. Not coincidentally, they occurred during the period (1981–85) in which British virtuoso guitarist Ray Flacke was in his band.

Raymond Flacke was born in Sussex, England, in 1951, and began playing the guitar at age 11 after being smitten with the instrumental Fender forays of Hank Marvin and the Shadows. A quick study, Flacke was gigging a year later, while digging on the heavy rock style of pre-Deep Purple Ritchie Blackmore. At one point Flacke played soul music in the Druids, appearing on one of their minor hits. He then spent five years in Germany playing twelve grueling hours a day with as many as twenty different bands. While there, in 1968, he saw a band of U.S. troops playing country music. The style intrigued him enough to further explore the genre in what would be a life-changing experience.

Back in London, Flacke was mightily impressed with the 1970 album *Area Code 615*, which featured crack Nashville session musicians like guitarists Wayne Moss and Mac Gayden. In addition, the records of Merle Haggard with his exceptional lead guitarist Roy Nichols alerted him to the deep well of magical sounds to be found in a Telecaster. Albert Lee, with *Head, Hands & Feet*, further alerted him to the potential of country-rock. In fact, when Flacke was playing the pub circuit, Lee would often sit in, much to Flacke's pleasure and edification. After years of backing other performers and doing studio gigs, Flacke finally mustered the courage to head across the big pond, landing in Nashville, in 1978. However, his real break would not come until 1980, when, while playing at the Wembley Music Festival in England, guitarist Ricky Skaggs caught Flacke's performance and enlisted him for his debut at the Grand Ole Opry.

Flacke became an in-demand session guitarist, beginning in the 1980s, playing with Travis Tritt, Mark McGuinn, Lacy J. Dalton, and Janie Fricke, among others. He recorded his first solo album, *Untitled Island*, in 1989. He then landed a plum gig touring with Marty Stuart and appeared on his 1991 release, *Tempted*. Around the same time, he began making instructional guitar videos. In 1993 he joined a group of fellow string-busters

Ray Flacke and his boss made a dynamic duo with their revolutionary combo in 1982 of traditional bluegrass and hot country pickin' on tunes like "Heartbroke" and "Don't Think I'll Cry."

including Jerry Douglas, Doc Watson, country bluesman John Cephas, and bluesy jazz cat Cal Collins on the "Master of the Steel String Tour." Ten years later, in 2003, Flacke exchanged his trusty Tele for a Guild D-60 and released the all-acoustic *Songs Without Words*, an album that has been described as "Julian Bream meets Jerry Reed."

How to Play It

Flacke's 16-measure solo is played over the same changes as found in the vocal verses (not shown). Despite the title of the song, it is not a blues progression, but instead a F#m–B7–E sequence with an amazing amount of musical information and a stunning climax.

After concluding the E major pickup measure, Flacke firmly establishes the F#m change in measure 1 with a whole-step bend from E to F#. Measure 2 is particularly instructive, as it contains a distinct characteristic of his style: triad substitution. Here, Flacke arpeggiates B and A triads over the F#m harmony; the move works because the notes of those triads are all contained in the F# Dorian mode. Flacke then continues with the same approach in measure 3, with G#m

and F#m triads employed over a B7 chord. In measures 5–8, the harmony shifts back to E major, so he works the E major scale with emphasis on the deep-talking bass strings. Be sure to pay attention to the repeating pull-off licks in measures 7–8, wherein Flacke creates a fluid, rolling legato phrase. Besides making for a logical conclusion to measures 1–8, in which the runs and licks descend from a higher to lower register, these bass licks by contrast set up the high-flying runs yet to come.

Flacke utilizes a more scalar concept in measures 9–12, leaning heavily on F# minor pentatonic (F#–A–B–C#–E) over the F#m chord, and then craftily slipping into the B Mixolydian mode (B–C#–D#–E–F#–G#–A) over B7. The real fun occurs in measures 13–16, where Flacke romps up the neck in sliding diatonic 3rds intervals, in a swinging eighth-note rhythm. This is one of Flacke's signature moves and a useful lick worth perfecting for future use. A large part of this lick's breathtaking effect is its rhythmic fluidity, generated by those baby-smooth slides. An efficient fingering system is necessary to insure a fast, smooth flow of notes. All of the fourth-string slides, or glisses, should be executed with the ring finger, while the note that follows on the third string should be played with either the index

finger (minor 3rds) or the middle finger (major 3rds).

Measure 16 presents a tricky fingering dilemma. Bend the B note at fret 16 with your middle or ring finger, and use your index finger to fret the following F# at fret 14. Then, on the second string, bend up a whole step at fret 17 with either your middle or ring finger, and then bend the A note at fret 17 with your ring finger. This may not be to everyone's taste, but it is the most efficient, given the tempo of the solo, and it is the way Flacke did it.

Vital Stats

Guitarist: Ray Flacke

Song: "Highway 40 Blues"

Album: *Highways and Heartaches* – Ricky Skaggs, 1982

Age at time of recording: 31

Guitar: Modified circa 1967 Fender Telecaster

1:47

Guitar Solo

Fast Country Shuffle ♩ = 231

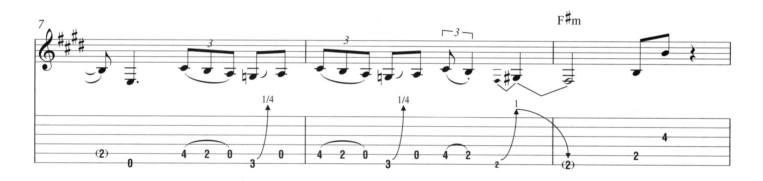

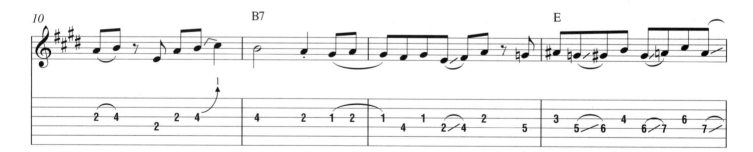

Words and Music by Larry Cordle

Jeff Cook

Alabama is the most popular country group of all time, breaking the accepted mold for the genre along the way. Traditionally, country bands were primarily backing bands for lead singers, but Alabama's cohesion as a unit, which owed much to Southern rock and pop music, changed that dynamic. That being said, their music clearly reflected roots in the honky-tonk Bakersfield sound as well as traditional, classic country music.

Formed in 1977, Alabama struck it huge in the 1980s, racking up twenty-one straight #1 country hits through 1987, and their forty-two #1 songs to date is a world record. With the distant cousins Randy Owen (lead vocals and rhythm guitar), Teddy Gentry (vocals and bass), and Jeff Cook (lead guitar, vocals, keyboards and fiddle) at the band's core, they were the first country group of note in many years to be a self-contained unit. Among their many accolades and awards are two GRAMMYs and a record twenty-three American Music Awards.

Guitarist Jeff Cook was born August 27, 1949, in Fort Payne, Alabama. As a youngster, his father and grandfather encouraged him to pursue music, so he took a few piano lessons. He was attracted to the guitar as well, with the Ventures being one of his influences, and by age 13 he was playing lead guitar and

"We played everything from Acuff to ZZ Top."

—Lead singer Randy Owen on their time at Myrtle Beach

Photo © 1988 McGuire

keyboards in his first band. Strongly drawn to the broadcast medium, Cook received his broadcast license three days after turning 14 and became a DJ at a local radio station.

Following his high school graduation, Cook pursued an electronics degree at Gadsden State Community College in Gadsden, Alabama. Along the way he found time to become proficient on banjo and mandolin, and in 1969 he formed the trio Young Country with Owen and Gentry. For their first gig, they won a high school talent contest playing Merle Haggard's "Sing Me Back Home" and were rewarded with a trip to the Grand Ole Opry in Nashville. When Cook and Owen finished college, the three moved to Anniston, Alabama, and shared an apartment, practicing their music at night and writing their first songs, including "My Home's in Alabama," while

working day jobs to pay the bills. In 1972, they changed the band name to Wildcountry and added a drummer. The following year they decided to go pro, and by 1974 had gone through four more

"Changes Comin' On," John Fogerty's classic "Green River," and "Gonna Have a Party" amply demonstrate how Jeff Cook bridged pop and country guitar with the best elements of both.

drummers as Cook added fiddle to his instrumental arsenal.

They changed their name again, in 1977, to the Alabama Band, later shortened to just Alabama, and signed a recording contract based on the strong following they had built in the Southeast. During the 1980s, Alabama had a total of twenty-seven #1 country singles, including "Mountain Music" (and a GRAMMY® for the album), along with seven multi-platinum albums. The band also crossed over to the pop charts nine times. In 1985, Cook won *Guitar Player* magazine's reader's poll for Best Pop Guitarist, and in 1998 the band received a star on the Hollywood Walk of Fame. Their popularity waned in the 1990s, and they broke up in 2003. Cook went on to form the eight-piece All-Star Goodtime Band with which he recorded three albums.

Besides other music projects outside Alabama, Cook designs and builds custom guitars and amps under the JCS and Stinger Musical Instruments brands. He also runs his own studio, called CookSound, and promotes the Chosen Few. In 2005 he and guitarist Mitch Glenn formed the duo Cook & Glenn to play country, soul, and rock 'n' roll featuring the All-Star Goodtime Band. Their self-titled debut is on Lofton Creek Records.

How to Play It

Lead singer Randy Owen recalls that "Mountain Music" was cut in two takes, as Alabama was well rehearsed. The results of their many years together and countless gigs reveal itself in the smooth tempo change that occurs in the song, as well as in Jeff Cook's short, economical, and imminently tasty solo.

Cook employs the A major pentatonic scale (A–B–C♯–E–F♯) over what is essentially an eight-bar D–A–D–A–G–D–A progression (the C♯m and F♯m chords serve as leading "kicks" into the D and G chords, respectively), to create licks more concerned with melody than the navigating of the changes. Notice that the progression, by featuring the D chord more prominently than the A chord, engenders an A Mixolydian tonality.

Cook plays primarily in tenth position, in what is colloquially known among blues guitarists as the "Albert King box," in measures 1–6. And though this is clearly not a blues progression, the compact scale position is advantageous for making "bluesy" bends within the major pentatonic framework. This is evident right from the pickup measure, where Cook bends the A up a whole step to B and then returns to a vibratoed A in measure 1. In measure 2 he returns to country form with a pedal steel–type oblique bend. The resulting harmony (E/C♯) represents the

5th and major 3rd intervals, respectively, of the underlying A chord. Bend the B note on string 2 at fret 12 with your ring finger backed by the middle and index fingers, and access the E note at fret 12 on string 1 with your pinky.

In measure 3, Cook uses a variation on his phrase from measure 1 to again support the D tonality. In measures 4–5 and the first two beats of measure 6, he relies heavily on another pedal steel–style bend and release, fitting over both G and D major chords. Part of the beauty of the major pentatonic scale is how well the notes harmonize with almost all the chords in a given key. In the second half of measure 6 and in measure 7, Cook presents oblique bends that reinforce the underlying D and A chord changes. Cook then changes his tactics in measure 8, injecting an A Mixolydian–based banjo roll lick that ends jaggedly with a quarter-step bend of the 6th (F♯), which leads back to the A major tonality of the coming verse.

Vital Stats

Guitarist: Jeff Cook

Song: "Mountain Music"

Album: *Mountain Music –* Alabama, 1982

Age at time of recording: 33

Guitar: Music Man Sabre II Double-Neck 6-string

Amp: Music Man

1:13

Track 16

Guitar Solo

Moderately ♩ = 114

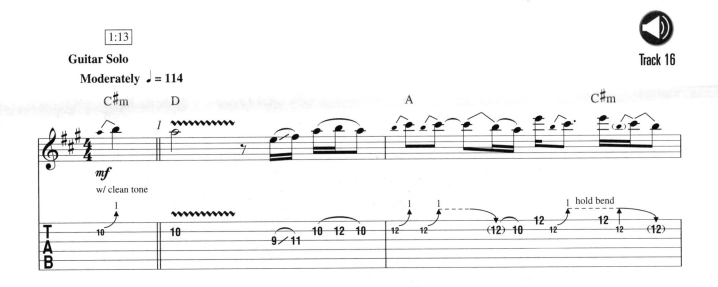

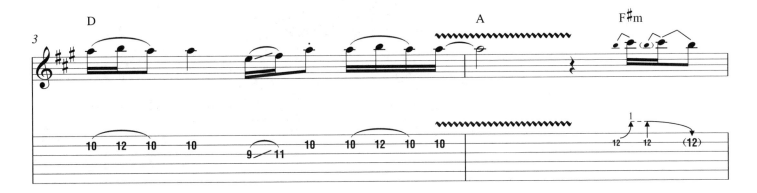

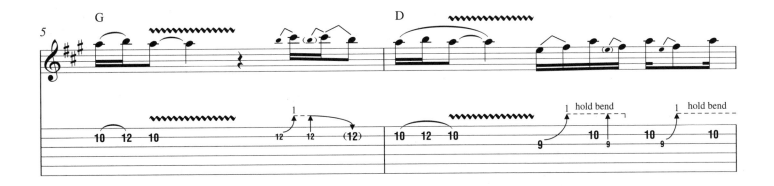

Words and Music by Randy Owen

Copyright © 1980 Sony/ATV Songs LLC
All Rights Administered by Sony/ATV Music Publishing, 8 Music Square West, Nashville, TN 37203
International Copyright Secured   All Rights Reserved

59

Reggie Young

That's the Way Love Goes, an album of sensitive ballads by the craggy Merle Haggard, peaked at #8 on the *Billboard* country album chart, in 1984. The album's title track had made it to #1 on the Hot Country Singles & Tracks chart, in 1983, winning the GRAMMY® for Best Male Country Performance, for Haggard's gentle reading of the old Lefty Frizzell classic featuring Reggie Young on lead guitar.

Reggie Young, whose resume includes over 590 album credits, may very well be the greatest country session guitarist of all time. The coral sitar parts on the Box Tops' "Cry Like a Baby" and B.J. Thomas's "Hooked on a Feeling" as well as the signature riffs on Dusty Springfield's "Son of a Preacher Man" and Dobie Gray's "Drift Away" are just a few of his creations. Young was born January 1, 1936, in Caruthersville, Missouri, but spent his early years in Osceola, Arkansas. His father played

Merle Haggard could not have picked a better "picker" to support his dour tales of woe as Reggie Young squeezes every ounce of sweet emotion out of "Carryin' Fire" and "If You Hated Me," among all others.

classical Hawaiian guitar and bought his son a National flat top for Christmas in 1950. A year later the family moved to Memphis, Tennessee, providing the 15-year old with the blues and R&B background that helped to inform his exceedingly tasty style via DJ Dewey Phillips (who helped to "break" Elvis) and the "Red, Hot & Blue" radio show. Likewise, hearing "Two Guitars" on Nashville's WSM, featuring Chet Atkins and Billy Byrd, informed his country music education. In 1955 Young joined Eddie Boyd and the Stompers and cut the hit "Rockin' Daddy," in 1956, followed by a tour with Johnny Cash, Roy Orbison, and Carl Perkins.

Young moved to Shreveport, Louisiana, in 1958, to back Johnny Horton on the "Louisiana Hayride," only to return to Memphis a year later. He joined the Bill Black Combo, and the instrumental group promptly had a hit with "Smokie"

in 1959. Led by Elvis Presley's original rockabilly bassist, they would go on to be voted the top instrumental group by *Billboard* magazine from 1960 to 1962, and opened for the Beatles on their first visit to the U.S., in 1964.

By the mid-1960s Young's exceptionally authentic R&B chops were finding their way onto recordings at Royal Studios in Memphis, FAME Studios in Muscle Shoals, Alabama, and Atlantic Studios in New York, where he backed Solomon Burke and Don Covay. Being a member

"He's the king and always will be, you know."

—Reggie Young on Elvis

of the Goldwax Records house band in Memphis led to him joining the "Memphis Boys" at Chips Moman's American Studios, where they made pop music history. Between 1967 and 1971, the same core of musicians played on 155 chart hits for an amazing list of artists ranging from Elvis Presley (to whom Young once offered constructive criticism in the studio and had it accepted) to Neil Diamond to Dean Martin.

Before moving west to Nashville in 1973, Young played on Danny O'Keefe's "Good Time Charlie's Got the Blues," and his smooth pedal steel–type licks eased his welcome into the studio scene in Music City. He backed another wide-ranging list of talent from B.B. King to Paul Simon while developing a special relationship with Merle Haggard that would last for years. In 1992 he joined up with the Highwaymen, including Waylon Jennings, Johnny Cash, Kris Kristofferson, and Willie Nelson, for a European tour. In 2005 Young reunited with Haggard on *Chicago Winds*. He continues to play sessions in Nashville, records with his wife, and also tours with original members of the Memphis Boys and Highwaymen, in addition to playing Elvis-themed shows around the world.

How to Play It

The seventeen-measure solo consists of two similar progressions: Eb–Bbm–Eb7–Ab–Bb–Ab–Eb–F7–Bb–Ab/C–Bb/D, and Eb–Bbm–Eb7–Ab–Bb–Ab–Eb–Bb–Eb–

Ab/C–Bb/D. To navigate the two choruses, Young uses the Eb major pentatonic scale (Eb–F–G–Bb–C) almost exclusively. Played in eighth position, you will probably recognize the scale pattern as being the same as the C minor pentatonic. The beauty of this approach is that it provides notes related to every one of the diatonic chords, while allowing the bluesy bends and phrasing common to the blues scale–type fingering.

Young sets the melodic tone of the solo by focusing on each measure's chord tones, beginning in measure 1 with the G and Bb notes (3rd and 5th, respectively, of the Eb major chord). In measure 2, he leans heavily on the F (5th of Bbm), with repeated whole step bends to G, which serve to anticipate the Eb7 that occurs on beat 3. Be aware that he picks only the first note of the legato-fueled phrase. The smoothness and fluidity with which Young executes the bends and releases is a hallmark of his vaunted style.

Over the Ab chord in measure 3, Young gently leans on the Eb (5th) in conjunction with the C (3rd). In measure 4, he uses the D (3rd) on beat 1 to herald the change to Bb, and climbs step-wise to the 5th (F), dressing it up with sweet vibrato. Measure 5's Ab chord finds Young once again nailing the Eb (5th), holding that focus in measure 6, to represent the root of the Eb chord. In measure 7, Young follows suit, focusing on the root, F, of the F7 chord. Showing his remarkable skill at maintaining forward momentum with minimal means, Young prominently bends the F to G in measure 8, in antici-pation of the Eb chord in measure 9. Check out that he repeats the licks from measures 2–4 in measures 10–12, in an

unusual move for an improvised solo but one that gives it cohesion and reinforces the vocal hook in an instrumental manner.

In measure 13, Young returns to his ad-lib approach, here emphasizing Eb (5th) and C (3rd) notes over the Ab chord. Heading towards the conclusion of his solo, he initiates a longer, bluesy, descending run in measure 14, creating musical tension with alternating C and Bb notes, starting on beats 3–4 and contin-uing into the first half of measure 16. Young continues down the scale, resolving to Eb on beat 1 of measure 16.

Vital Stats

Guitarist: Reggie Young

Song: "That's the Way Love Goes"

Album: *That's the Way Love Goes* – Merle Haggard, 1983

Age at time of recording: 47

Guitar: 1969 Fender Telecaster

Amp: Fender Concert

That's the Way Love Goes

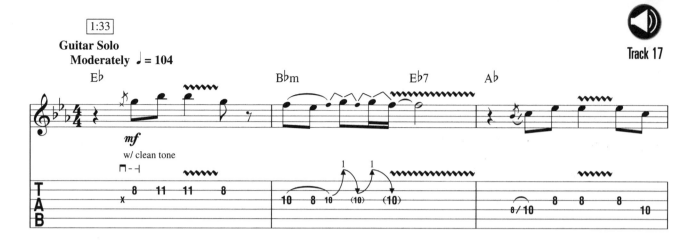

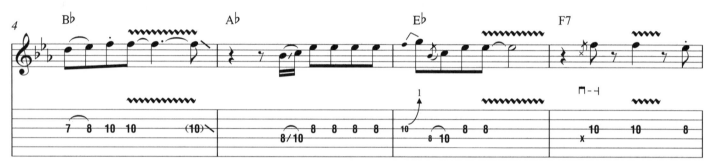

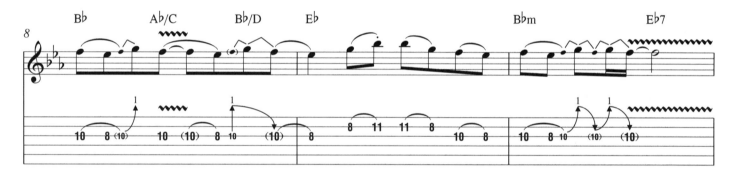

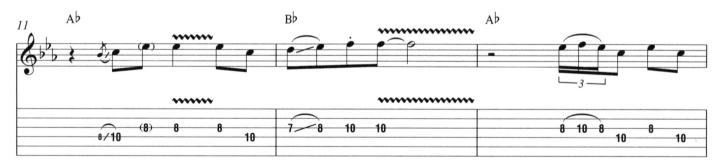

Words and Music by Lefty Frizell and Sanger Shafer
Copyright © 1973 by Peer International Corporation and Sony/ATV Songs LLC
Copyright Renewed
All Rights on behalf of Sony/ATV Songs LLC Administered by Sony/ATV Music Publishing, 8 Music Square West, Nashville, TN 37203

Pete Anderson

"What would Freddie King do?"

—Anderson describing his approach to soloing on *Guitars, Cadillacs, Etc., Etc.*

In a genre that does not care much for real mavericks like Hank Williams, Merle Haggard, and Buck Owens in their early years, country rebel Dwight Yoakam eventually managed to find his niche with the Nashville faithful. With his producer and partner-in-crime, country blues-rocker Pete Anderson, Yoakam helped pioneer "cowpunk" music, in the 1980s, while still managing to crack the country music Top 10 on occasion and selling wagon-loads of records, to boot.

Guitarist Pete Anderson was born in 1952, in Detroit, where he first heard the country and western music his father favored, before being turned on to rock 'n' roll when he saw Elvis Presley perform on the "Ed Sullivan Show," in 1956. Eventually he would be drawn to Detroit's urban blues sounds (John Lee Hooker), and then later to Chicago blues immortal Muddy Waters. Around 1960 he got a Hawaiian guitar, but his interest in and ability to play sports won out until a friend played Bob Dylan's 1965 release *Bringing It All Back Home*, with the revolutionary, subversive blues-rock of "Subterranean Homesick Blues." At the age of 16, with newfound passion, he

bought a guitar and a Dylan songbook and played in a number of rock bands, including a jug band at age 17, but it was the blues that fired him up then and continues to do so now.

After graduating high school, in 1970, he bummed around the country, attended art school, got married, and settled down to a life of working in the Detroit factories during the day while gigging at night. Anderson moved to Los Angeles in 1972, where he played not only rock and blues but also the country music of his youth. In 1979, he enjoyed some success with Rick Tucker & the Good-Time Band, based in part on the popularity of the movie *Urban Cowboy*. Still, financial security eluded Anderson, so he painted houses during the day, which finally enabled him to send for his wife and child. The late 1970s also saw Anderson enroll at the new Guitar Institute of Technology, to further his musical education.

Meeting Dwight Yoakam in the early 1980s would provide Anderson with his meal ticket. The two forged a lasting relationship that has not only allowed him to play with but also produce for the charismatic young cowboy rocker. Following a stint in the Babylonian Cowboys, they became the darlings of the L.A. alt-country crowd and signed with Warner/Reprise in 1985. A year later, *Guitars, Cadillacs, Etc., Etc.* would go platinum while firmly establishing Yoakam's career. *Hillbilly Deluxe* followed in 1987, reaching #1 on the country charts and containing four Top

Courtesy of www.peteanderson.com

10 hits, including "Please, Please Baby." That same year, Anderson took a short break from working with Yoakam and was briefly replaced by Eddy Shaver. Bouncing back, Anderson and Yoakam would take great pride in "Streets of Bakersfield," their first #1 hit, in 1988, as they were able to lure Buck Owens out of

Pete Anderson comes to play his Tele with bluesy passion as he fires up Elvis's "Little Sister," "Smoke Along the Track," and "This Drinkin' Will Kill Me."

retirement to sing. Anderson has also played with and produced for a wide range of artists from Michelle Shocked, Roy Orbison, and Lucinda Williams to the Meat Puppets, K.D. Lang, and Rosie Flores. In 2000 Anderson and Yoakam collaborated on the all-acoustic *dwightyoakamacoustic.net* featuring Yoakam playing solo acoustic guitar. His twentieth record, *Blame the Vain* (2005), was Yoakam's first without Anderson.

In 1993 while still with Yoakam, Anderson formed Little Dog Records to produce various other worthy artists as well as his own solo recordings *Working Class* (1994), *Dogs in Heaven* (1997), and most recently, *Daredevil* (2004). He has also released an instructional video titled *Roots Rock Workout* (Warner Home Video).

How to Play It

All the great country guitarists have uniqueness and individuality, but Pete Anderson breaks free of the pack in a significant way on "Please, Please Baby." Resisting the temptation to blast out hot licks and singe the strings of his Tele, he opts instead to play tasty blues licks over the sixteen-measure boogie progression in the key of E.

With a few notable exceptions at the climax of his solo, Anderson utilizes the E composite blues scale (E–F#–G–G#–A–Bb–B–C#–D) in several positions. Measures 1–6 contain classic country-blues licks in open position. Observe the tangy blues-powered G/C# double stop bent up one quarter step in measures 1 and 4. This classic move creates hot musical tension that resolves to an open E/B double stop. In measure 5, Anderson drives the tension higher, alternating C/G double stops in seventh position with G/D double stops in second position, with open E/B stabs in between.

In measures 7–10, Anderson begins to address each chord change with specific scales and harmony. In measures 7–8, he turns a twelfth-position descending double stop pattern into a harmonious moment with motion, as it leads nicely to some dynamic mandolin-type strumming of the unison E notes in measure 9. After a gliss to the eighth-fret G note on beat 1 of measure 11, Anderson returns to the open-position E composite blues scale.

Just in case Anderson feared alienating Yoakam's hardcore country fans with his trip deep into the blues, he pours on the country sounds in measures 13–16. In measure 13, he employs 6ths from the B major scale to firmly establish the tonality with some juicy diatonic harmony. Then, in measures 14–16, he tosses off a sensational chromatic pattern comprising open strings as well as 6ths and assorted other harmonies, climbing from fret 4 all the way up to fret 16, capping his solo with a G#/B (7th/9th) double stop over the A chord that starts the next verse. Anderson uses hybrid picking throughout the solo, but it is absolutely essential for this climactic conclusion.

Vital Stats

Guitarist: Pete Anderson

Song: "Please, Please Baby"

Album: *Hillbilly Deluxe* – Dwight Yoakam, 1987

Age at time of recording: 40

Guitar: 1959 Fender Telecaster Custom

Amp: Fender Deluxe Reverb blackface

Please, Please Baby

Track 18

Guitar Solo
Moderately fast Country Shuffle ♩ = 160

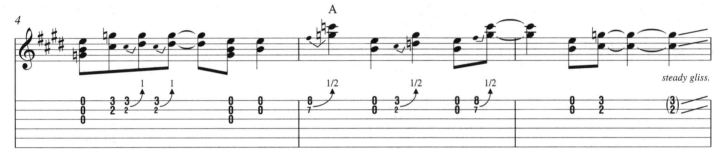

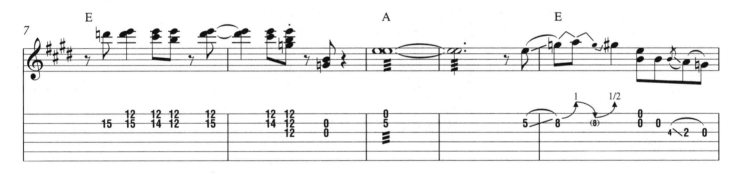

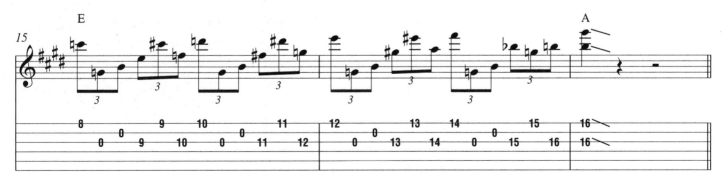

Steady gliss.

Danny Gatton

Photo by Ron Pownall/Michael Ochs Archives/Getty Images

"If I turn it up all the way it doesn't need reverb."

----Gatton referring to his Fender Bassman

Danny Gatton, nicknamed "The Humbler" by Amos Garrett and hailed as "the world's greatest unknown guitarist" by the music community, arguably had more chops than any guitarist in any genre. With seemingly little effort he mastered everything from blinding chicken pickin' lines to a good-natured parody of heavy metal shred. Though he was shy onstage, he was nonetheless an entertainer; for instance, after playing slide with a beer bottle, he would wrap a towel around the neck of his Tele and still play cleanly and accurately through the fluffy material. Ultimately, his eclectic tastes and lack of vocal ability and songwriting skills would prove his commercial undoing, as he watched countless other guitarists not worthy of changing his strings climb far higher on the ladder of success.

Daniel Wood Gatton, Jr. was born to Norma and Daniel on September 4, 1945, in Washington, D.C. At age 6 the youngster heard the recordings of Les Paul, and he was hooked. He was naturally left-handed but played guitar right-handed, a decision that would prove to account for some of his amazing dexterity. By age 12 he could play Les Paul and Mary Ford's version of "How High the Moon." At the same time, he was absorbing the influences of jazz guitar great Charlie Christian and rockabilly pioneer Scotty Moore as well. Like many guitarists, such as John Fogerty from Creedence Clearwater Revival would later do, he copped Bill Doggett's "Honky Tonk" with its classic solo by Billy Butler, even as his supportive parents exhorted him to "play a million miles an hour." In 1960, he joined the Offbeats, and when they broke up after four years, he headed south to Nashville for a fruitless shot at the studios. As would occur throughout his abbreviated recording career, he was just too eclectic and progressive for the conservative elements of the music business.

By 1968, Gatton was back in the D.C. area and gaining a rabid local following, as was his friend and fellow Tele-master, Roy Buchanan. Virtually every guitarist passing through town, including British blues bangers like Savoy Brown's Kim Simmonds, would regularly make pilgrimages to attend their legendary performances in two-bit dives. Buchanan was even known to make Gatton leave a pay phone off the hook at his gigs, so he would not miss what his "competition" was putting down.

Superlatives become superfluous when describing the unmatched virtuoso Danny Gatton throughout this album, but especially on "Blues Newburg," "Fandingus," and "Slidin' Home."

In 1974, Gatton formed Danny and the Fat Boys, cutting *American Music* in 1975 and *Redneck Jazz* in 1978. When they disbanded he took a break from performing, including a sojourn to Santa Cruz, California, until he was asked to play on a Commander Cody record. Dates with country star Roger Miller and then neo-rockabilly idol Robert Gordon followed; however, having to "play down" with Gordon sent the virtuosic Gatton into a depressive funk, and he withdrew from the national stage yet again.

In 1989 Gatton unleashed his devastating chops on *Unfinished Business* on his own NRG label, named for his mother Norma. When Elektra Records came knocking and insisted, quite logically, that he *only* play instrumentals, it appeared that at last he was being recognized for his unparalleled prowess and allowed to flourish in the arena he knew best. *88 Elmira St.* (1991), which wisely showcases his arrangements and towering technique on the Beach Boys' "In My Room" and "The Simpsons Theme," along with seven original numbers, charted at a modest #121. Gatton got to indulge his "jones" for jazz on *New York Stories* (Blue Note), in 1992, but when *Cruisin' Deuces* (Elektra, 1993), an album similar to *88 Elmira St.*, stiffed, he was dropped from their roster. A collaboration with Hammond B-3 maestro Joey DeFrancesco resulted in the intriguing yet ultimately incomplete *Relentless* in 1994. The death of his rhythm guitarist, Billy Windsor, and the cumulative weight of his career disappointments collided on October 4, 1994, when, following a domestic dispute, he locked himself in his garage and committed suicide, leaving a bereaved adolescent daughter, wife, and mother, along with countless fans worldwide.

How to Play It

"Elmira St. Boogie," named for his birthplace in Washington, D.C., showcases Gatton's chops in a boogie blues setting that has roots back to early postwar "hillbilly boogie." As opposed to his instrumental versions of popular vocal tunes, with conventional verses and choruses, this tune has several different sections identified by rehearsal letters. Rehearsal letter B functions as an improvised solo and comprises four eight-measure quadrants for a total of thirty-two measures, arranged in the standard AABA American song form.

The A progression, found in measures 1–8, 9–16, and 25–32, comprises an E7–A9–B–E7 progression. Gatton had a tremendous toolbox of improvisational tools at his disposal, which, combined with his substantial jazz influences, allowed him to navigate chord changes with impressive variety. In measures 1–4, he utilizes double stops culled from the E composite blues scale (E–F#–G–G#–A–Bb–B–C#–D) for musical texture. An ascending run up the B major pentatonic scale (B–C#–D#–F#–G#) in measures 5–6 gooses the momentum, while the open-position E7 chord tones in measures 7–8 provide dynamic contrast and twang.

Measures 9–11 give a tantalizing taste of the vaunted Gatton flash, with laser-precision E composite blues pull-offs in twelfth position. Observe how the notes work over both the E7 and A7 changes while generating massive musical tension. Next, check out the classic blues riff in measure 14, including the cool b3rd–3rd (D–D#) hammer-on at beat 3. Even hipper are the quarter-step bends applied to the

G/D double stops in measure 15, implying the tart E7#9 tonality (known euphemistically as the "Hendrix chord," as heard in "Purple Haze").

In the B section (measures 17–24), Gatton shifts gears and parlays chordal forms throughout for a dynamic change of pace. Take note of how he indicates the change from A9 to E simply by raising the open G note in measures 17–18 and 21–22 to G# in measures 19–20, while maintaining the open E/B dyad on the top two strings. Then, at the return to the A section, in measures 25–32, Gatton ups the ante by picking E notes across *four octaves* over an implied E chord, and a similar form over the first bar of the subsequent A change, and finally calling on a series of triple stops and double stops to close out the boogie romp.

Vital Stats

Guitarist: Danny Gatton

Song: "Elmira St. Boogie"

Album: *88 Elmira St.*, 1991

Age at time of recording: 46

Guitar: 1954 Gibson ES-295

Amp: 1963 Fender Vibrolux

Elmira St. Boogie

0:57

Guitar Solo

Fast Rockabilly ♩ = 180

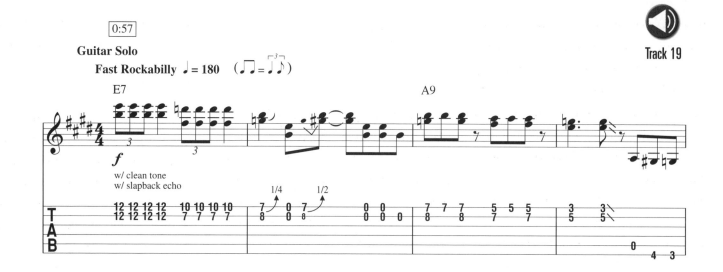

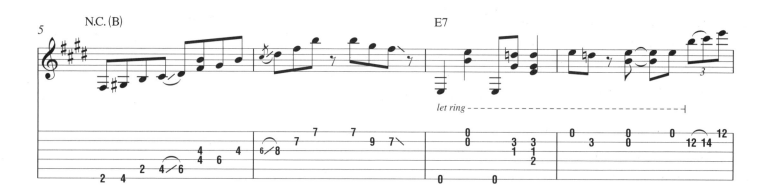

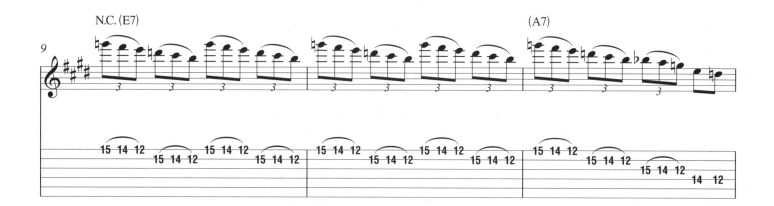

Composed by Danny Gatton

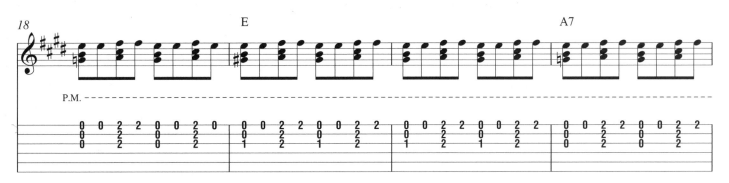

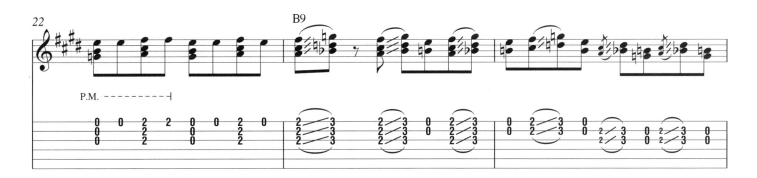

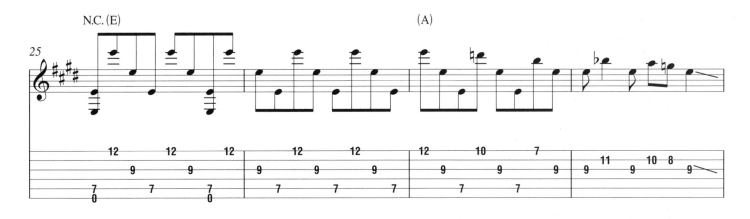

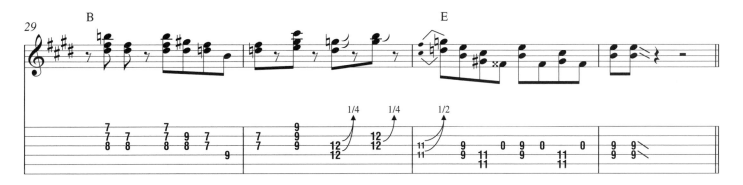

Wendell Cox and Richard Bennett

Travis Tritt had already separated himself from the pack in the 1980s by *not* wearing a cowboy hat—black or otherwise—when his presciently titled second album *It's All About to Change* went multi-platinum and reached #2 on the country charts and #22 on the *Billboard* pop charts in 1991. More important than his sartorial decisions, however, were his blues influences (check out his cover of Buddy Guy's "Homesick") and his decision to use two great session guitarists to create maximum instrumental excitement on the record—an absolute must in that era of modern country music.

One of those two guitarists was Wendell Cox. Born April 29, 1965, in Cumming, Georgia, he picked up his mother's Gibson Hummingbird flat-top acoustic at age 13 and played along to the recordings of the Atlanta Rhythm Section and Lynyrd Skynyrd. In a matter of weeks he asked for and received a 1968 Gibson Les Paul goldtop from his harmonica-playing father. At 15, Cox joined a band called First Ade with his brother, and then the group Special Edition. Though he left the latter to get married, a former band mate recommended him to Travis Tritt in 1990. Cox and Tritt hit it off immediately as both had Southern blues-rock in common. Cox aced the audition and has played with Tritt for eighteen years, last appearing on *The Restless Kind* in 1996. After a break, he is again touring with Tritt, and is currently playing in a project called Big Hammer, with singer Jim Jenness.

The other half of Tritt's dynamic duo, Richard Bennett was born in Chicago on July 22, 1951. He heard his first country music as a young boy in the 1950s, on radio station WJJD. In 1960 he moved to Phoenix, Arizona, and began studying the guitar with western band leader Forrest Skaggs. Bennett eventually became friends with Al Casey (not to be confused with R&B guitarist Al Casey

Courtesy of www.richard-bennett.com

"May his crackling guitar find a place in your heart, as it has in mine."

—Mark Knopfler
on Richard Bennett

who played with Fats Waller), who was then a top Hollywood session guitarist and veteran of Skaggs's band. This relationship led to his first gigs, in 1968, when he spent a summer vacation with Casey. Bennett moved to the west coast in 1969 and quickly found studio work with a diverse range of artists such as Peggy Lee, Liberace, and the Ventures, as well as country legends like Tennessee Ernie Ford. In 1971, he landed a gig with Neil Diamond that would last for a productive seventeen years and sixteen albums.

Photo by Robb D. Cohen/Retna Ltd.

"The guitar kept me from going out and finding trouble."

—Wendell Cox

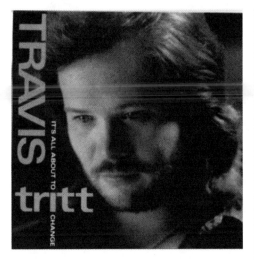

"If Hell Had a Jukebox" and "Homesick," among others, thrillingly show the double trouble guitar duo in flat-out Southern rock mode.

Bennett began commuting to Nashville in 1982, and at Steve Earle's advice, relocated there in 1985. When he played on and co-produced Earle's landmark *Guitar Town*, in 1986, it opened the door to a career as a noted producer, working with such greats as Emmylou Harris and Marty Stuart, among many others. In 1994, his career took another direction when he began playing and recording with Mark Knopfler (Dire Straits), in a relationship that continues unabated. In 2004 Bennett released a solo album of instrumentals called *Themes for a Rainy Decade* and joined his friend Vince Gill in the Notorious Cherry Bombs, who had once backed Emmylou Harris in the early 1980s.

How to Play It

Cox and Bennett play relay team guitarists in their 16-measure solo, in which each runs with the baton for eight short measures. Cox covers his segment of G–C7–G–D chord changes with the G composite blues scale (G–A–B♭–B–C–D♭–D–E–F). The whole-step bends from A to B (the exceedingly sweet 3rd of G) in measure 1 is a characteristic of the best modern Nashville electric guitarists. Cox also injects a healthy dose of pedal steel–type harmony with the fretted D note on string 2 picked in conjunction with the open G string in measure 2. Measure 3 may be the hippest of all, however, as he turns the notes from a C7 chord into a rich, melodic riff that simultaneously adds a bit of flash.

In measures 4–6, Cox sails up the fingerboard with smooth precision through the G Mixolydian mode (G–A–B–C–D–E–F), with the addition of tart blues bends from A to B♭ in measure 5 and from E to F in measure 6. The descending 6ths in measure 7 contribute welcome harmony, texture, and contrast to the preponderance of single-note lines. Just as importantly, it provides a smooth transition back to the third-position G composite blues shape for the conclusion of his solo. See that his last note, G, on string 4 at fret 5, is notated in *divisi* at the start of Bennett's solo, in measure 9.

Richard Bennett does his "dangest" to imitate a pedal steel guitar in the first three measures of his solo, with a descending series of oblique bends that resolves to a G/D dyad over the G chord in measure 4. The sequence is quite brilliant in the way it focuses heavily on chord tones to match the underlying G and C chords. The following fingering system is recommended in order to execute the licks as fluidly as Bennett: First of all, keep your pinky finger planted on the first-string note throughout. For the bends in measure 9, use your middle finger on the second string. For the bends in measure 10 and the first beat in measure 11, use your ring finger on string 2. When the bends change to string set 3–2, on beat 2 of measure 11, use your middle finger to bend the third string, while holding down the second-string notes with your ring finger.

Bennett makes a dramatic shift in register and technique for measures 5–8, as he winds down the solo on the resonant bass strings—not unlike one of his influences, the immortal "king of twang," Duane Eddy. Here, he employs the open-position G composite blues scale as the source for his flowing, melodic licks characteristic of the best of country guitar. Notice too how measures 4–8 of Bennett's solo contrast with measures 4–8 of Cox's solo, as each guitarist opts to complement the other without encroachment or duplication.

Vital Stats

Guitarists: Wendell Cox and Richard Bennett

Song: "Here's a Quarter (Call Someone Who Cares)"

Album: *It's All About to Change* – Travis Tritt, 1991

Ages at time of recording: Cox 26; Bennett 40

Guitars: Gibson Les Paul (Cox); Fender Stratocaster (Bennett)

Here's a Quarter (Call Someone Who Cares)

0:58

Guitar Solo

Rowdy Country Waltz ♩ = 114

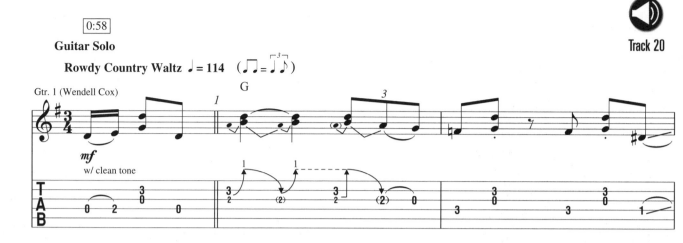

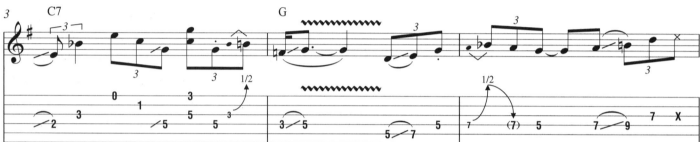

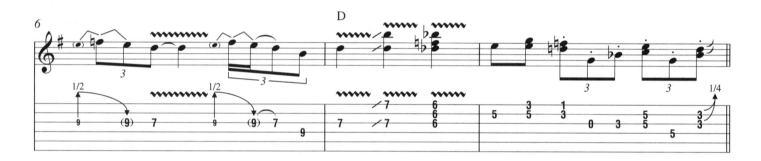

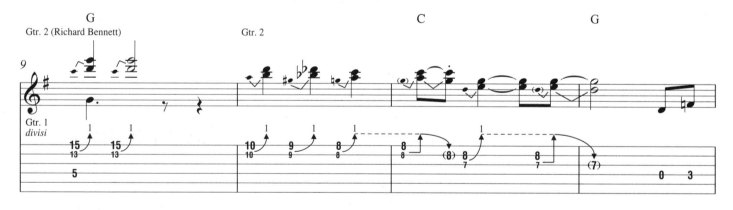

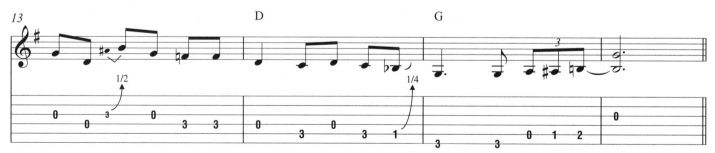

Words and Music by Travis Tritt

Brent Mason

"Constantly reinvent yourself if you want any longevity in your career."

—Advice given to Mason by Chet Atkins

Alan Jackson was part of the posse of young bucks who helped revitalize Nashville in the 1990s with a healthy dose of blues, honky-tonk, and rock 'n' roll. He was second only to Garth Brooks in popularity, and his clean-cut looks and friendly demeanor contributed to his ability to maintain a loyal fan base. During the first twelve years of his recording career, he scored a remarkable twenty #1 country singles—with twenty

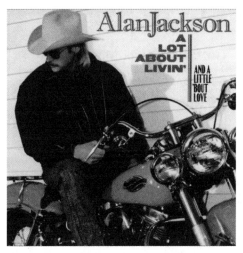

What made Brent Mason in-demand as a top session cat is his telepathic ability to play for the song while goosing the energy with his distinctive instrumental voice as on "Chattahoochee" and "She's Got the Rhythm (I've Got the Blues)."

others reaching the Top 10—while providing steady employment for the virtuosic and prolific guitarist Brent Mason. Though the venerable Harold Bradley, in his fifty years on the scene, has been generally regarded as the most-recorded guitarist in history, Mason has already doubled his output in just twenty-two years of plying his trade on Nashville's Music Row.

Brent Mason was born on July 13, 1959, in Van Wert, Ohio. A child prodigy, he began playing the guitar at age 5, sliding a kitchen knife across the strings of his father's acoustic, and soon had his musical family members form a band around him and his brother Randy (drums). Chet Atkins, Hank Williams, Merle Haggard, Ernest Tubb, Roy Nichols, and Jerry Reed were his country influences, though his eclectic tastes extended to Ray Charles, George Benson, Stevie Wonder, James Taylor, and Jeff Beck. Mason played in a number of rock bands in high school and took a job in a toolbox factory, where he saw fellow workers lose hands and suffer other mangling injuries. When he punched a hole through his thumb one day with a rivet machine, he realized it was time to give his music its full due, so he quit and moved to Nashville in the late 1970s. When his demo tapes failed to attract the desired attention, he reluctantly returned to Ohio and a factory job. When both he and his wife were laid off, however, they

Courtesy of Brent Mason

headed back to Music City for a second try, in 1981. With help from pedal steeler Paul Franklin, Mason latched on to the house band at the Stagecoach Lounge, a gig that would support him for the next five years.

Around 1984, Chet Atkins stopped by the Lounge to check out Mason, as the band had built an enviable buzz. "Mr. Guitar" was sufficiently impressed to return with George Benson for a second look. Convinced of Mason's talent,

Atkins invited him to play on *Stay Tuned* (1985), an album that also featured "Bad Benson," Jeff Beck, Mark Knopfler, Larry Carlton, Steve Lukather, and Earl Klugh, among others, swapping licks with the master.

Before long, Nashville's best were beating a path to Mason's door for his songs as well as his hotshot guitar chops. Clint Black, Brooks & Dunn, Glen Campbell, Neil Diamond, Faith Hill, Waylon Jennings, George Jones, Don McLean, Reba McEntire, George Strait, Randy Travis, Tanya Tucker, Steve Wariner, Shania Twain, and Trisha Yearwood are only some of the most prominent artists to benefit from his string work. His guitar was also heard on commercials for products ranging from Michelob to Betty Crocker, as well as on movie soundtracks and TV themes. Recognition also came in the form of awards, including the Academy of Country Music naming him "Guitarist of the Year" every year from 1993 to 1998, the Country Music Association's "Musician of the Year" award in 1997 and 1998, and *Music Row* magazine presenting him with the "Top 10 Album All Star Guitarist" award 1995–99. In 1997 Mason released his solo debut album, the GRAMMY-nominated, all-instrumental *Hot Wired*, with a guest appearance from Chet Atkins. And in 2006 he was one of the first to be inducted into the Musicians Hall of Fame in Nashville. The same year he released *Smokin' Section*, with his brother Randy on drums.

How to Play It

This classic "car" blues was originally written and recorded in 1949 as "Mercury Boogie," by Bay Area bluesman K.C. Douglas. Born in Mississippi and influenced by the Delta blues of Tommy Johnson, with whom he later performed, Douglas relocated to Northern California just after World War II. David Lindley and Steve Miller covered the tune before Jackson, and the Ford Motor Company later purchased the rights to use it in commercials.

Brent Mason mixes a sweet stew of country music and blues licks on "Mercury Blues." He forges his solo over a 12-bar blues progression in D, with a Bm (vi) substitution in measure 9 that makes for a subtle but significant harmonic change. This move is often heard in jazz, but less often in the blues and almost never in honky-tonk country music. One of the results is that Mason and the other soloists take a different tack during that measure. (Note: For this song, Mason tunes his sixth string to D to enhance his rhythm accompaniment, but he does not use the string during the solo.)

In measures 1–4, Mason accelerates through the open-position D composite blues scale (D–E–F–F#–G–Ab–A–B–C). In addition, check out the pedal-point dyads that open measure 3. Including chords or chord partials in a solo is a country-guitar characteristic that goes all the way back to Maybelle Carter's groundbreaking work in the 1930s.

In measures 4–5, Mason eases into the G Mixolydian mode (G–A–B–C–D–E–F) with a classic banjo-roll move into a killer pedal steel–style oblique that reinforces the underlying G major tonality while also providing dynamic contrast to the quick single-note lines. In measure 7, Mason heralds the D chord change with a bluesy "train-whistle" double stop before snaking down the D composite blues scale.

As previously mentioned, for the Bm chord in measure 9, Mason departs from the standard country approach of minor and major pentatonic scales, to impart some of his jazz influences via a slick B melodic minor (B–C#–D–E–F#–G–A#) ascent. He then immediately snaps back into the honky-tonk with a sassy pre-bend on string 3, releasing from C# to B, and resolving to A, to reinforce the V chord (A) tonality. Revving into high gear, he continues with a spicy dash of chicken pickin' in measure 11, before closing the solo with some tasty pedal steel–style double stop moves.

Vital Stats

Guitarist: Brent Mason

Song: "Mercury Blues"

Album: *A Lot About Livin' (And a Little 'Bout Love)* – Alan Jackson, 1992

Age at time of recording: 33

Guitar: Modified 1968 Fender Telecaster

Amp: Fender Twin Reverb

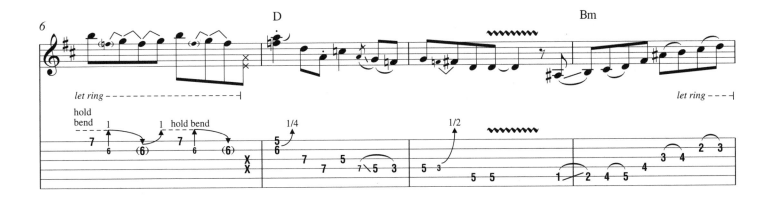

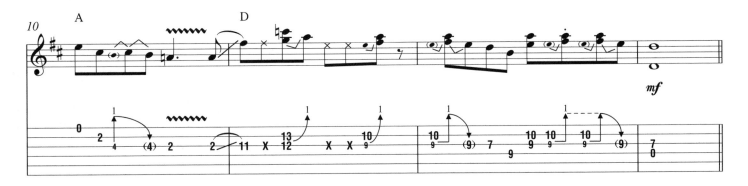

Vince Gill

Photo © David Atlas/Retna Ltd.

"Yeah, I'm an old blues hound… to me we're all just blues singers and blues players."

——Vince Gill

Vince Gill's bio reads like it could be the lyrics of a classic country song about "movin' on" and the "cheatin' side of life." Indeed, the man has paid his dues and remains a survivor on the Nashville scene. He has won eighteen Country Music Association awards—more than anyone else—and is tied with Chet Atkins, at fourteen, for most GRAMMYs by a country artist.

Vincent Grant Gill was born in Norman, Oklahoma, on April 12, 1957, to Stanley J. and Jerene. He studied violin and piano as a child, and his father, who was an amateur country musician, encouraged him to use his talent and pursue a musical career. So the young Gill took a few guitar lessons around age 13, eventually learning mandolin, fiddle, dobro, and bass on his way to becoming a true multi-instrumentalist. By 14 he was playing lead guitar and played in several groups throughout his school years, including a high school bluegrass band called Mountain Smoke that once opened for Pure Prairie League. Upon graduation, in 1975, Gill moved to Louisville, Kentucky, where he played bass and guitar briefly with Ricky Skaggs and Jerry Douglas in Boone Creek before moving west to Los Angeles, where he joined noted fiddler Byron Berline's band Sundance, to mostly play mandolin. In 1979, he went to an audition for Pure Prairie League, mainly to see if they would remember him and his old band, and he ended up getting the gig as their lead singer. Three albums and a Top 10 hit later, he was off to join the Cherry Bombs, Rodney Crowell's band, in 1981, before signing a deal with RCA in 1983.

Gill moved to Nashville, where following in the footsteps of his illustrious predecessors Ricky Skaggs, Albert Lee, and James Burton, he began doing session work and touring with Emmylou Harris, while also working on his own material. A couple of singles and albums later, he left RCA Records and signed with MCA, in 1989. The move turned out to be a wise one, as his MCA debut, *I Call Your Name*, won a GRAMMY® for the title track, and the second single, "Never Knew Lonely," went to #3 as the album sold more than a million copies. Mark Knopfler asked him to join Dire Straits, but Gill saw his star rising and declined. *Pocketful of Gold* (1991) was

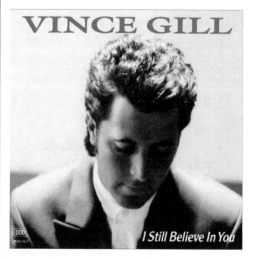

With kudos from Mark Knopfler and Eric Clapton, it is expected that Vince Gill can pick it with the best of them, and he does not slack off on "One More Last Chance" and "Pretty Words."

aptly named, as it also went platinum, but his breakout album was *I Still Believe in You* (1992), which likewise went platinum and spawned four #1 hits: "I Still Believe in You," "Don't Let Our Love Start Slippin' Away," "One More Last Chance," and "Tryin' to Get Over You."

Success followed Gill throughout the 1990s, including his first #1 country album, *The Key* (1998), which was an autobiographical account of the breakup of his marriage to Janis Oliver, former singer with the Sweethearts of the Rodeo. His career hit a bump in 2000, however, when he married Christian music singer Amy Grant following a period of rumors about their having a romantic relationship while she was still married to singer and songwriter Gary Chapman. Gill's resulting autobiographical album, *Let's Make Sure We Kiss Goodbye*, sold well but was critically panned as being maudlin and sentimental. He bounced back, however, with his self-produced *Next Big Thing* (2003), which snared a GRAMMY® for the title track. Feeling discouraged due to a lack of radio play, a phone call from Eric Clapton inviting him to play at the Crossroads Festival in 2005 inspired a writing frenzy that became the epic four-disc *These Days*, which won a GRAMMY® for the single "Reason Why," in 2006. In 2007 Gill and his fellow famous Oklahoman, songwriter Jimmy Webb, wrote and performed the single "Oklahoma Rising" for the two-disc, forty-six-track *Oklahoma Rising*, a tribute to the state centennial.

How to Play It

Gill's seventeen-measure solo is, for practical purposes, sixteen measures, with the last measure functioning as a pickup back into the verse. Listen to the original recording and you'll hear that Gill uses more compression on his guitar than most of his country music peers, resulting in a fatter, sustained sound that still maintains the desired Fender twang.

Gill is a fan of the Mixolydian mode, and his use of it over major chords (as opposed to dominant chords) imparts a bluesy flavor that is very much a part of his style. Witness his D Mixolydian (D–E–F♯–G–A–B–C) lines over the D chord in measures 1–2 and 4–6. However, in measures 9–10, 12, and 14–17, Gill covers the D major harmony with the D composite blues scale (D–E–F–F♯–G–A♭–A–B–C), to add a bit of snappy bark to his bluesy bite.

Over the G chord in measure 3 Gill pulls out some G Mixolydian (G–A–B–C–D–E–F) chicken pickin' to contrast the more fluid runs in the preceding measures. In measures 11 and 13, also over a G chord, he maintains his G Mixolydian tack, only this time he plays in lower register, for smooth transition from and into the D changes that surround it.

The A chord only appears in measures 7–8 and 15, and Gill takes advantage of the situation by throwing a melodic curveball. In measure 7, he fires up the fifth-position A minor pentatonic scale (A–C–D–E–G) and gets down and gritty with a whiny unison bend before slapping in a classic blues run that resolves to A in measure 8. He then anticipates measure 9's D change with a lick from the D minor pentatonic scale (D–F–G–A–C) on beats 3–4. In measure 15, Gill adds a nice descending chromatic move that side-slips right into the final D chord.

As befits a "closet bluesman," Gill exercises his bending chops in the solo. Though most are of the typical whole-step variety, be sure to see the spicy quarter-step bends peppered throughout that tickle the ear with their bluesy dissonance.

Vital Stats

Guitarist: Vince Gill

Song: "One More Last Chance"

Album: *I Still Believe in You*, 1992

Age at time of recording: 35

Guitar: 1953 Fender Telecaster

Amp: Blackface Fender Super Reverb

Track 22

Guitar Solo

Moderately fast ♩ = 180

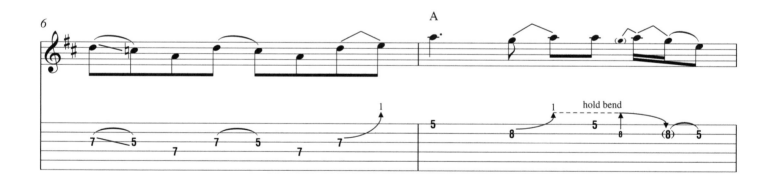

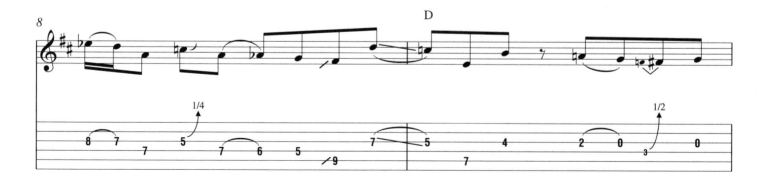

Words and Music by Gary Nicholson and Vince Gill

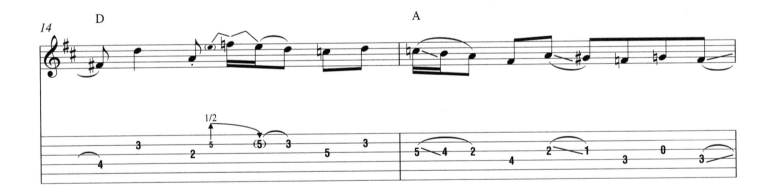

In a genre enthralled with virtuoso string manipulation on Fender Telecasters, it was only a matter of time before a trio of super-pickers playing nothing but instrumentals, often in three-part harmony, would come into scary existence. The cleverly named Hellecasters, featuring guitarists John Jorgensen, Jerry Donahue (see "The Claw," page 83), and Will Ray, got together in 1990 for a series of fun, one-off gigs at the legendary Palomino Club. The audience response was so overwhelming, however, that along with the offer for a record deal from former Monkee Mike Nesmith, the trio decided to stick around and form something more permanent. Their debut, the wryly titled *The Return of the Hellecasters* (1993), was a cause for celebration for guitar freaks of all persuasions. The awards and accolades poured in as the Hellecasters gladly and gleefully provided a musical orgy of bends, slides, harmonics, and volume swells all in the service of the almighty *twang*. As an appreciation for the invaluable publicity and as a means to recognize the unsurpassed musical accomplishment of the three guitarists, Fender Musical Instruments has produced seven signature-model guitars for the band, a record for the company.

Will Ray stands out as a devastating Tele-basher, even among his esteemed colleagues in the band and the many other virtuosos who "spank the plank." (Note: Ray has since switched to G&L guitars, founded by none other than Leo Fender and his old partner George Fullerton). Ray was born in Richmond, Virginia, in 1950, and at the age of 10 he heard the music of Elvis Presley,

Leadbelly, and folk acts like Peter, Paul & Mary through his older brothers and sisters. The great guitar music of the Beatles, Cream, the Rolling Stones, and the Butterfield Blues Band would catch his ear in the 1960s, but he would not begin to play until he was 16. He then spent countless hours learning the hot licks of Eric Clapton, Mike Bloomfield, Keith Richards, and Danny Kalb of the Blues Project.

Ray put the guitar aside after high school and joined the Army for a two-year tour of duty that included a stint in Vietnam. He then went to college on the GI bill in the early 1970s. In his sophomore year, he heard the Grateful Dead's 1969 *Live/Dead* album, which inspired him to become totally immersed in the guitar via marathon practice sessions. Upon graduation he was in and out of a number of Richmond bands, including the country rock outfit King Cotton. By the time he joined the straightahead country band the Pacers, he was hooked on the pedal steel licks of Roy Buchanan, James Burton, Clarence White, and Danny Gatton.

In 1983, Ray split for the Los Angeles studio scene, where he first came in contact with inventor Dave Borisoff and his B-bender, a mechanical device retrofitted to a solidbody guitar that stretches the B string, thus allowing for more accurately and authentically emulated pedal steel licks. He would become so enamored with the device that he installed B-benders on all his axes.

An embarrassment of riches for guitarists of all stripes, Will Ray and his cohorts will blow you away on "Orange Blossom Special" and "Menage: The Beak/The Claw."

Ray played in a number of bands in the emerging genre called "cow punk," including the Vanishing Breed, Tin Star, Candye Kane & the Armadillo Stampede, and Will Ray and the Gila Monsters. In 1992, he was named Guitarist of the Year by the California Country Music Association. While producing a contemporary country compilation album of local talent called *Hollywood Roundup* he met and played with Jerry Donahue and John Jorgensen. The rest is history. After their acclaimed 1993 album *Return of the Hellecasters*, they released *Escape from Hollywood* in 1995, followed by *Hell 3: New Axes to Grind* in 1998. Ray released his solo LP *Invisible Birds* the next year and *Mojo Blues* in 2001, and continues to play with his buds in the 'Casters while also producing for bands like the Buzzards and giving guitar clinics.

How to Play It

Ray takes a wild ride over the relatively brief eight-measure G–D–C–D–G–D–C–B7 progression—relatively brief because the "Hellecaster Theme" has a double-time feel that makes the 120 bpm tempo feel like a NASCAR time trial. Ray makes the best of his short time in the spotlight, however, using his B-bender and a slide in conjunction with conventional fretting to create a fast, fluid cascade of sumptuous tones and technique.

As opposed to the main themes of the song, and even the solos of John Jorgenson and Jerry Donahue, Ray makes very deliberate scale changes to follow the harmonic progression. In measures 1–5, he uses slippery pedal steel licks that focus on chord tones to nail each bar's underlying harmony. If you do *not* have a B-bender equipped guitar, these licks require you to execute whole-step bends with your fret hand's *index* finger (ouch!). Also, if performing these bends with your finger, you'll need to change fret locations to make a few of them work. For example, to execute the two bends that commence on beat 3 of measure 2, you'll need to shift the notes down a string set, so that the stationary D note is played with your pinky on the fourth string at fret 12, and the bend from E to F♯ is performed with your index finger on the third string at fret 9. As you work through these licks, focus on nailing the intonation and smooth, fluid execution.

In measure 6, Ray uses a slide to dance on the G and B strings in 17th position. These double stops in 3rds are a cornerstone of playing slide in standard tuning because they are on parallel strings at the same fret position and therefore more practical to access with the slide.

However, observe how Ray angles his slide to access the double stop on beat 4, a necessity in standard tuning for minor 3rds in the scale. Amazingly, he sometimes wears ring slides on *both* hands for a full-on, frontal assault on the senses!

Ray next shifts to the G major scale (G–A–B–C–D–E–F♯) for a classic descending sequence in 3rds, with an open B string separating each dyad. Do not miss how he moves one-half step from G/E on beat 2 of measure 8 to resolve the B7 chord with an F♯/D♯ (5th/3rd) dyad on beat 3.

Vital Stats

Guitarist: Will Ray

Song: "Hellecaster Theme"

Album: *Return of the Hellecasters*, 1993

Age at time of recording: 43

Guitar: Fender Telecaster with B-bender

Amp: Matchless DC-30

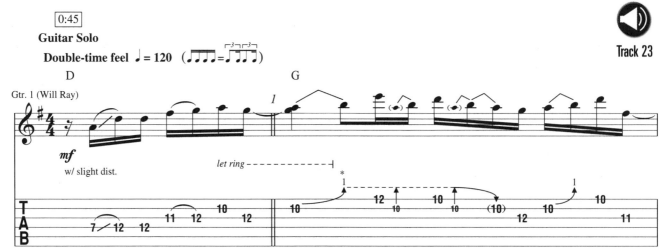

*All bends played w/ B-bender. Let bends ring throughout.

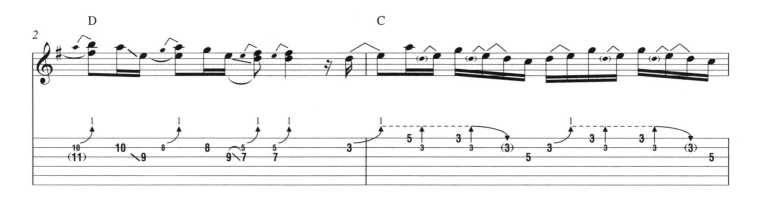

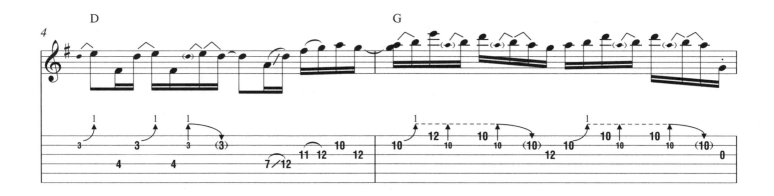

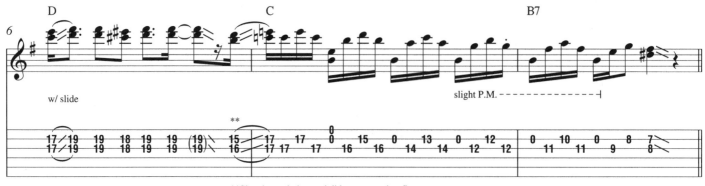

**Slant bar technique w/ slide worn on ring finger.

Written by John Jorgenson
© 1993 JORGENSONGS (BMI)/Administered by BUG MUSIC
All Rights Reserved   Used by Permission

Jerry Donahue

"The string-bending king of the planet."

—The late Danny Gatton's accolade for Donahue

Jerry Donahue was born in New York, New York, on September 24, 1946. His father Sam was a big-band leader, tenor saxophonist, and trumpeter best known for his time with the swing bands of drummer Gene Krupa, clarinetist Benny Goodman, and trombonist Tommy Dorsey. His mother, Patricia, was a film and television actress. As you can see, Donahue did not exactly experience the humble beginnings that are the stuff of country music legends. The piano got Donahue's attention when he was but a wee lad of 5. As he grew up in the 1950s,

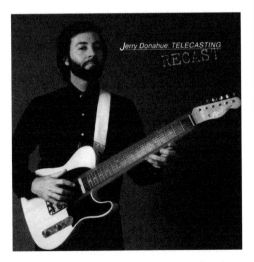

"Medley: Snowflake Reel/Toss the Feathers/ Red-Haired Boy/The Cherokee Shuffle" practically says it all in elucidating Jerry Donahue's width and breadth of superb talent.

however, he was guided to take classical guitar lessons, and eventually came under the pervasive influence of Chet Atkins as well as "twang-meister" Duane Eddy, the Ventures, Chuck Berry, and the Fireballs. He did not begin to play in earnest until 1960, however, when he overheard country great Gerry McGee pickin' 'n' grinnin' on the Sunset Strip in Los Angeles. It was his first encounter with string bending, and from that moment, his life would never be the same.

In 1961, the 14-year old Donahue moved to England to further his education in yet one more example of how circuitous his journey was in becoming one of the acknowledged modern masters of the Telecaster. While there, he discovered the clean Stratocaster sound of Hank Marvin and the Shadows, Great Britain's answer to the Ventures. His impeccable taste in guitar heroes would later evolve to include James Burton, Roy Buchanan, Jerry Reed, Clarence White, Amos Garrett, Eric Clapton, Albert Lee, and Richard Thompson, whom he would replace in Fairport Convention. Significantly, he developed an interest in Celtic music combined with his American roots, thereby closing the circle, as British folk music is the basis of the earliest country music. In the process Donahue would forge a unique style and sound admired by his peers and fans alike.

Photo by Marty Temme

From the 1960s through the 1980s, an impressively long series of folk, country, and rock artists enjoyed Donahue's contributions, in performance or on record. A select list would include Poet and the One Man Band, Fotherngay with singer Sandy Denny (whom he would join in Fairport Convention), former Spooky Tooth singer/keyboardist Gary Wright, Johnny Hallyday, Ian Mathews, Fairport Convention, Joan Armatrading, Michelle Phillips, Gerry Rafferty, Ralph McTell, Linda Thompson, Robert Plant and Friends, Warren Zevon, Roy Orbison, Bonnie Raitt, George Harrison, and the Yardbirds. The "Theme from Catlow," in 1972, was his first instrumental outing under his own name, while his prized first solo release, *Telecasting*, appeared in 1986.

In 1991 Donahue, along with two other underground legends, Will Ray and John Jorgensen, would finally break free of his cult status. The trio of virtuosos banded together to form the aptly titled Hellecasters. Their debut album, *The Return of the Hellecasters* (Rio Records, 1993), along with *Escape from Hollywood* (1994), and *Hell 3: New Axes to Grind* (1997) are a veritable orgy of bends, slides, open-string pull-offs, careening harmonics, and volume swells. The Hellecasters short "commercial" run was a welcome antidote to the era's pop music, which seemingly downplayed instrumental excellence of any kind. The guitar press responded accordingly, lavishing awards and rave reviews upon the terrible trio. Not missing a golden promotion opportunity, Fender Musical Instruments responded with signature model guitars for the group, including, in a first for the company, both Tele and Strat models for Donahue. (Currently he is an endorsee of Peavey and their Omniac JD signature-model guitar.) The Hellecasters continue gigging, as the members' various schedules permit.

Donahue has remained busy as an in-demand session guitarist by stretching his strings and chops for, among others, the Animals. His landmark *Telecasting* was reissued in 1999 as *Telecasting Recast*, on the heels of *Brief Encounters* (1997), *Neck of the Woods* (1992), and *Meetings* (1988).

How to Play It

Jerry Donahue's knuckle-busting instrumental theme song combines the head from Jerry Reed's equivalent showcase "The Claw" (1967) and a forty-eight-measure solo all his own doing ("The Beak"). Consisting of eight six-measure choruses of A–D–A–E–D–A chord changes that resemble a compressed blues progression, it is a virtuoso performance that has his fingers nearly flying off the neck.

In measures 1–6, Donahue immediately establishes that he is going to draw on the inherent melodic qualities of the A major scale (A–B–C#–D–E–F#–G#) and the funk of the A blues scale (A–C–D–E♭–E–G), leavened with liberal doses of chromatic lines. The chromatic-cum-6ths lick in measures 1–2, an Albert Lee classic, conveniently serves as exhibit A. To nail it, alternate pick the chromatic lines on string 3, and use your middle finger to snap the notes on string 1. Sticking with the A hybrid scale, Donahue also pays attention to the changes, making sure to emphasize the important chord tones over each under-lying chord. The latter can be seen in measure 5, where Donahue emphasizes the E note over the E chord, and then C and A notes (♭7th and 5th, respectively) over the D change.

Donahue trots out one of his many famous tricks in measure 7, where he raises the pitch of string 4 by pushing down on it *behind* the nut! In order to replicate this advanced technique you will need a Telecaster-style guitar, where the string height behind the nut is suffi-cient to generate a whole step raise in pitch. You also need to make sure that your D string slides freely in its slot in the nut, and it might be easier if the slot has a spot of graphite or some other non-greasy lubricant to help. You will also need a good ear to judge the pitch accu-rately.

Every chorus in "The Claw" is a miracu-lous mini-composition with a beginning, climax, and end. However, if one section were to be singled out for special commendation it would be measures 36–42. In measures 36–37, Donahue nimbly ascends the A major scale, with an added ♭7th (G), in a fluid sliding motif on the top two strings that sounds like amplified raindrops falling on a meadow. He then mirrors the move, in measures 40–41, with an equally slippery and largely chromatic descent on strings 3–4, closing the phrase with a twangy bass-string move in measure 42. Sheer bliss.

Vital Stats

Guitarist: Jerry Donahue

Song: "The Claw"

Album: *Telecasting Recast*, 1998

Age at time of recording: 52

Guitar: Fender Telecaster

Amp: Sessionmaster JD-10

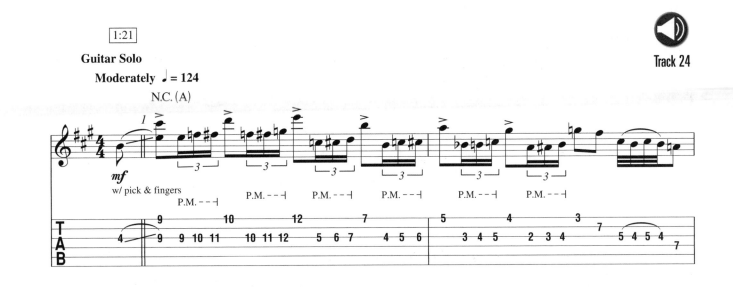

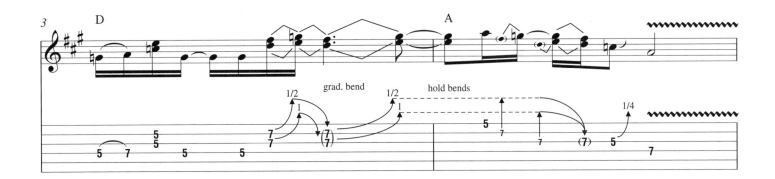

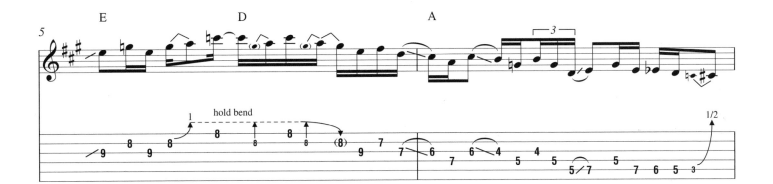

*Bend behind nut.

By Jerry Reed

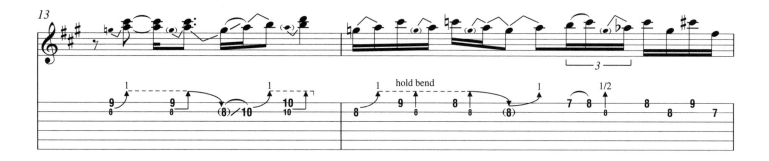

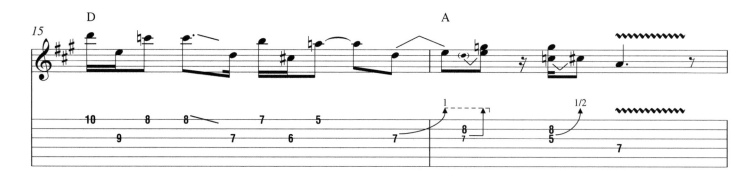

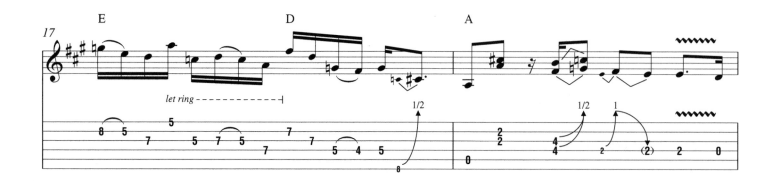

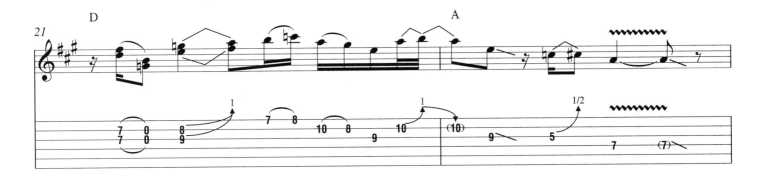

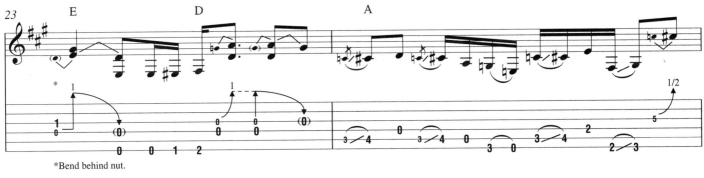

*Bend behind nut.

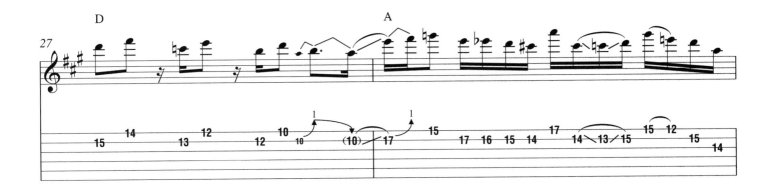

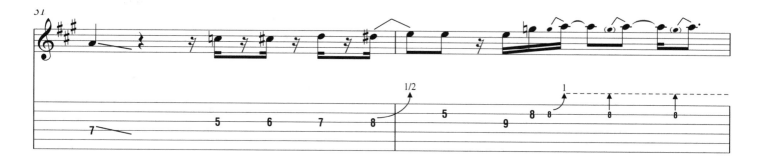

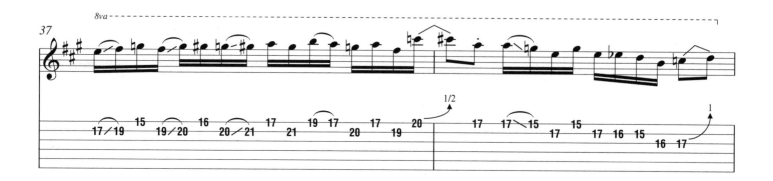

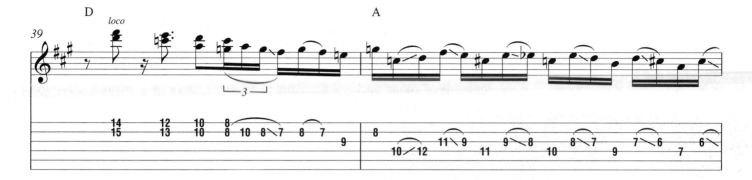

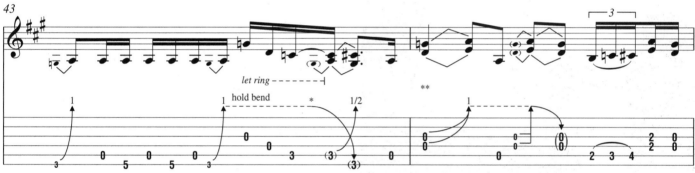

*While bending low E string, catch A string with the same finger.
While releasing bend, continue to depress A string, causing its pitch to raise.

**Bend behind nut.

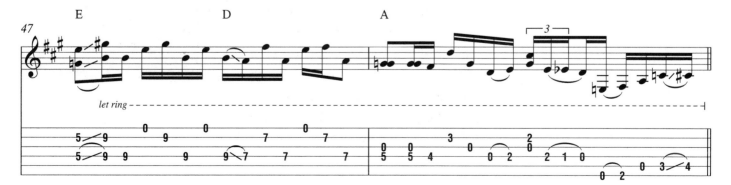

Brad Paisley

Photo by Marc Morrison/Retna Ltd.

"Anything that's going wrong in your life, you can pick this guitar up and it will go away."

—Warren Jarvis,
Paisley's grandfather

Country music legend George Jones calls him the "torchbearer for traditional country music," and as the latest in a long line of young buckaroos looking to leave his mark on MOR contemporary country music with a classic mix of honky-tonk and western swing, Brad Paisley may be the best yet. Not coincidentally, he is also the closest to being a flat-out rocker, though still fiercely loyal to his country roots. Wiry and charismatic with a square jaw and menacing chops, he also stands the best chance of seriously crossing over to the pop audience should he desire.

Brad Douglas Paisley was born October 28, 1972, to Sandy and Doug, in Glen Dale, West Virginia. His maternal grandfather, Warren Jarvis, played guitar and provided eight-year old Paisley with his first inspiration as well as his first instrument—a Sears Silvertone with the amp in the case. Exposure to grand-dad's favorites—Merle Travis, Chet Atkins, and Les Paul—along with his innate talent, led to rapid progress for Paisley, and by the age of ten he was performing in his church and local fraternal organizations. The exceptionally young prodigy formed Brad Paisley and the C-Notes with his guitar teacher Hank Goddard, and after an executive at West Virginia radio station WWVA heard his first original song, "Born on Christmas Day," the 12-year old was invited to appear on "Jamboree USA." He would become a regular on the Saturday night show for the next eight years, playing with established artists like Roy Clark and Little Jimmie Dickens.

After high school, Paisley enrolled in local West Liberty College before transferring to the Belmont University music business program in Nashville. The move would prove invaluable as he met not only his future producer but also a songwriting partner and several future band mates. A college internship at ASCAP led to him being offered a songwriting deal with EMI Music Publishing upon graduation. Upon hearing one of his many demos, Arista Records signed Paisley to a contract, in 1999, the same year he made his first of forty Grand Ole Opry appearances. His debut album, *Who Needs Pictures*, went platinum in 2000, while "He Didn't Have to Be" became the first of nine singles to hit #1.

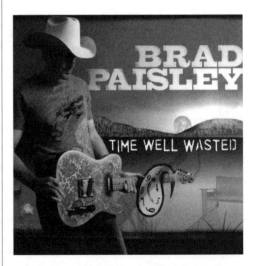

"Time Warp" and "Cornography" decisively proclaim to "The World" that Brad Paisley can duke it out on six-string with any of his illustrious contemporaries.

He won the Country Music Association Horizon Award and the Academy of Country Music award for Best New Male Vocalist. His first GRAMMY® nomination arrived in 2001, for Best New Artist. In 2002, he released his sophomore effort, *Part II*, which contained his third #1 single, "I'm Gonna Miss Her (The Fishing Song)."

In 2003, his third album, *Mud on the Tires*, became his first #1 country album, on the strength of his singles "Celebrity," which reached #31 on the *Billboard* charts, and "Whiskey Lullaby" with Allison Krause, which hit #41. For guitar fans, the album also contains Paisley duking it out on a duet with sharp-shooting guitarist Redd Volkaert, on "Spaghetti Western Swing."

Time Well Wasted (2005), however, conclusively showed Paisley's estimable and growing technique with the stunning instrumental "Time Warp." The album, featuring the rocking "The World" (#45) as well as "When I Get Where I'm Going," with Dolly Parton, and "Out in the Parking Lot," with Alan Jackson, reached #2 on the *Billboard* charts. It also won the CMA award for Album of the Year.

In 2006 Paisley released a Christmas album of covers and originals, and in 2007 he put out *5th Gear*, his fifth straight album to garner gold, going #1 country and nominated for three GRAMMYs. Fully in command of the lead guitar chair at this point, he is poised to take his place next to such hot country guitar heroes as James Burton, Albert Lee, and Ray Flacke.

How to Play It

Paisley flat-out blitzes through the sixteen-measure solo in "The World." A knowledgeable scale man, stemming in part from his study of Hank Garland, he utilizes a variety of spellings to negotiate the E–B–C#m–A–E–B–C#m–D–A progression. In measures 1–2, Paisley plays thump-and-stutter octave E notes on the bass strings, making the transition from the honky-tonk boogie rhythm of the verse take off like a rocket. In measures 3–4, he switches to double stops culled from the B Mixolydian mode (B–C#–D#–E–F#–G#–A), ending on a swooping one step bend of an E/B dyad to F#/C#. Continuing along with impeccable taste, Paisley dips into the ninth-position C# blues scale (C#–E–F#–G–G#–B) in measures 5–6. Observe, however, that in measure 6 he includes the major 7th (B#; enharmonically notated as C) and ♭9th (D), for a subtle but hip jazzy touch. Paisley then nails the A chord in measures 7–8 with the second-position A Mixolydian mode (A–B–C#–D–E–F#–G), like a good ol' country picker.

In measures 9–10, Paisley "gets down" with an E composite blues scale (E–F#–G–G#–A–B–C#–D) phrase on the bass strings in open position for a sound that harkens back to measures 1–2. For easiest execution, use hybrid picking for this phrase. Beginning in measures 11–12, however, he starts to take his solo "out" with a variety of improvisational

tools jammed into the two measures. In measure 11 he gets going with a run from the B composite blues scale that leads to a chromatically-fueled double stop phrase that climbs to the tonality-defining F#/D# dyad on the "and" of beat 2 in measure 12. On beat 3, Paisley anticipates the upcoming C#m change with an E–G#–E move that buys just enough time to shift up to seventh position, where he bends an A note up to B, the bluesy ♭7th of C#m. He then follows with a run down the C# minor scale (C#–D#–E–F#–G#–A–B), hitting the bluesy ♭5th (G) along the way. Adhering to the changes, Paisley nails D major scale tones over measure 14's D chord, though he phrases them as if playing from the twelfth-position E composite blues scale. Having planned ahead, or reacting intuitively on the spot, he remains in 12th position and hammers out 3rds-based double stops for a big-bang end of "The World."

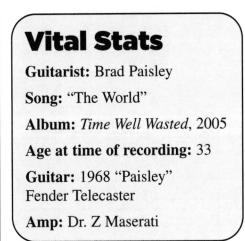

Vital Stats

Guitarist: Brad Paisley

Song: "The World"

Album: *Time Well Wasted*, 2005

Age at time of recording: 33

Guitar: 1968 "Paisley" Fender Telecaster

Amp: Dr. Z Maserati

2:27

Guitar Solo

Moderately fast ♩ = 180

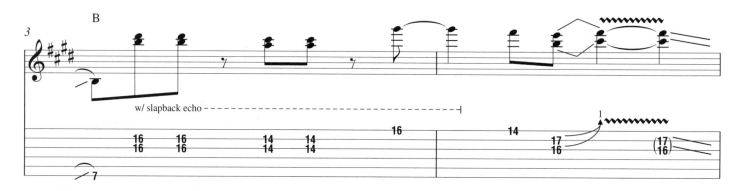

Track 25

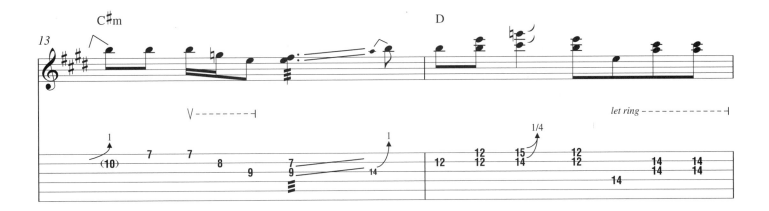

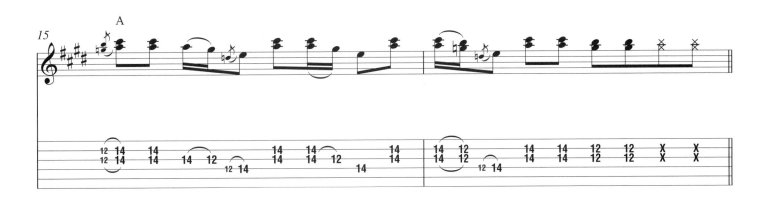

Conclusion

More than the other classic American music genres of the blues, jazz, and rock, *country* music has remained true to its core audience of southern and rural folks. The result is a consistency of form and content even as it evolves and the baton is passed to succeeding generations. And, while societal changes may occur more rapidly now than, say, fifty years ago, the traditional values still inherent in country music are reassuring to its audience, which has not only outgrown its original regional boundaries, but national ones as well.

The reward for guitarists, in particular, has been a wellspring of new sounds, techniques, and even instruments. It is worth noting, for example, that the iconic country electric guitar, the Fender Telecaster, was specifically designed for country guitarists by unapologetic fan Leo Fender. The first commercially viable whammy bar, as developed by Paul Bigsby for Merle Travis and refined by Fender for his Stratocaster, was conceived to imitate pedal steel guitar effects characteristic of country music. Likewise, banjo-picking patterns and fiddle tunes have long been adapted by country guitarists as part and parcel of their style.

Will the future bring similar ground-shaking innovations in country guitar? If history is any indicator, anything is possible. The pride that comes with achieving musical excellence, pride that goes back to country's roots in the Appalachians, burns bright as ever in a new generation that is open to innovative sounds and musical ideas.

About the Author

Dave Rubin is a New York City blues guitarist, teacher, author, and journalist. He has played with Son Seals, Honeyboy Edwards, Chuck Berry, Steady Rollin' Bob Margolin, Billy Boy Arnold, Johnny Copeland, James Brown's JBs, and the Campbell Brothers, among others. In addition, he has performed on the *Blues Alley* TV show in Philadelphia and *New York Now* in New York City and has appeared in commercials for Mountain Dew and the Oreck company.

Dave has been an author for the Hal Leonard Corporation for 20 years and currently has nine titles in his *Inside the Blues* series to go along with his numerous *Signature Licks* and *Guitar School* series and other assorted titles. He was the musical director for Star Licks DVD series *Legends of the Blues* and *Johnny Winter Legendary Licks Slide Guitar* instructional DVD for Cherry Lane Music. His *12-Bar Blues* book/DVD package (Hal Leonard) was nominated for a Paul Revere Award in 1999.

As a journalist, he currently writes for *Guitar Edge* and has written for *Guitar One, Living Blues, Blues Access, Guitar School, Guitar Shop, Guitar, Guitar Player,* and *Guitar World* magazines. Dave was the recipient of the 2005 Keeping the Blues Alive award in journalism from the Blues Foundation in Memphis, Tennessee.

Guitar Notation Legend

Guitar music can be notated three different ways: on a *musical staff*, in *tablature*, and in *rhythm slashes*.

RHYTHM SLASHES are written above the staff. Strum chords in the rhythm indicated. Use the chord diagrams found at the top of the first page of the transcription for the appropriate chord voicings. Round noteheads indicate single notes.

THE MUSICAL STAFF shows pitches and rhythms and is divided by bar lines into measures. Pitches are named after the first seven letters of the alphabet.

TABLATURE graphically represents the guitar fingerboard. Each horizontal line represents a string, and each number represents a fret.

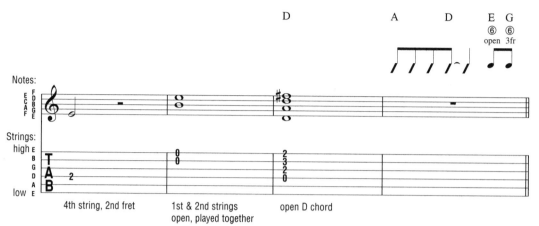

4th string, 2nd fret

1st & 2nd strings open, played together

open D chord

Definitions for Special Guitar Notation

HALF-STEP BEND: Strike the note and bend up 1/2 step.

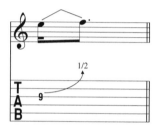

WHOLE-STEP BEND: Strike the note and bend up one step.

GRACE NOTE BEND: Strike the note and immediately bend up as indicated.

SLIGHT (MICROTONE) BEND: Strike the note and bend up 1/4 step.

BEND AND RELEASE: Strike the note and bend up as indicated, then release back to the original note. Only the first note is struck.

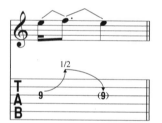

PRE-BEND: Bend the note as indicated, then strike it.

PRE-BEND AND RELEASE: Bend the note as indicated. Strike it and release the bend back to the original note.

UNISON BEND: Strike the two notes simultaneously and bend the lower note up to the pitch of the higher.

VIBRATO: The string is vibrated by rapidly bending and releasing the note with the fretting hand.

WIDE VIBRATO: The pitch is varied to a greater degree by vibrating with the fretting hand.

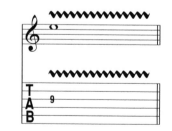

HAMMER-ON: Strike the first (lower) note with one finger, then sound the higher note (on the same string) with another finger by fretting it without picking.

PULL-OFF: Place both fingers on the notes to be sounded. Strike the first note and without picking, pull the finger off to sound the second (lower) note.

LEGATO SLIDE: Strike the first note and then slide the same fret-hand finger up or down to the second note. The second note is not struck.

SHIFT SLIDE: Same as legato slide, except the second note is struck.

TRILL: Very rapidly alternate between the notes indicated by continuously hammering on and pulling off.

TAPPING: Hammer ("tap") the fret indicated with the pick-hand index or middle finger and pull off to the note fretted by the fret hand.

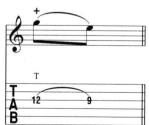

NATURAL HARMONIC: Strike the note while the fret-hand lightly touches the string directly over the fret indicated.

PINCH HARMONIC: The note is fretted normally and a harmonic is produced by adding the edge of the thumb or the tip of the index finger of the pick hand to the normal pick attack.

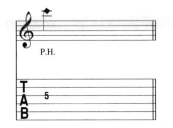

HARP HARMONIC: The note is fretted normally and a harmonic is produced by gently resting the pick hand's index finger directly above the indicated fret (in parentheses) while the pick hand's thumb or pick assists by plucking the appropriate string.

PICK SCRAPE: The edge of the pick is rubbed down (or up) the string, producing a scratchy sound.

MUFFLED STRINGS: A percussive sound is produced by laying the fret hand across the string(s) without depressing, and striking them with the pick hand.

PALM MUTING: The note is partially muted by the pick hand lightly touching the string(s) just before the bridge.

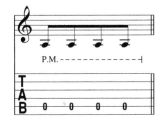

RAKE: Drag the pick across the strings indicated with a single motion.

TREMOLO PICKING: The note is picked as rapidly and continuously as possible.

ARPEGGIATE: Play the notes of the chord indicated by quickly rolling them from bottom to top.

VIBRATO BAR DIVE AND RETURN: The pitch of the note or chord is dropped a specified number of steps (in rhythm), then returned to the original pitch.

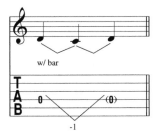

VIBRATO BAR SCOOP: Depress the bar just before striking the note, then quickly release the bar.

VIBRATO BAR DIP: Strike the note and then immediately drop a specified number of steps, then release back to the original pitch.

Additional Musical Definitions

(accent)	• Accentuate note (play it louder).	
(accent)	• Accentuate note with great intensity.	
(staccato)	• Play the note short.	
⊓	• Downstroke	
V	• Upstroke	
D.S. al Coda	• Go back to the sign (𝄋), then play until the measure marked "*To Coda*," then skip to the section labelled "**Coda**."	
D.C. al Fine	• Go back to the beginning of the song and play until the measure marked "*Fine*" (end).	

Rhy. Fig.	• Label used to recall a recurring accompaniment pattern (usually chordal).
Riff	• Label used to recall composed, melodic lines (usually single notes) which recur.
Fill	• Label used to identify a brief melodic figure which is to be inserted into the arrangement.
Rhy. Fill	• A chordal version of a Fill.
tacet	• Instrument is silent (drops out).
	• Repeat measures between signs.
	• When a repeated section has different endings, play the first ending only the first time and the second ending only the second time.

NOTE: Tablature numbers in parentheses mean:
    1. The note is being sustained over a system (note in standard notation is tied), or
    2. The note is sustained, but a new articulation (such as a hammer-on, pull-off, slide or vibrato) begins, or
    3. The note is a barely audible "ghost" note (note in standard notation is also in parentheses).

Guitar Instruction
Country Style!
from Hal Leonard

CHICKEN PICKIN' • *by Eric Halbig* **INCLUDES TAB**

This book provides a "bird's-eye-view" of the techniques and licks common to playing hot, country lead guitar! Covers over 100 hot country guitar licks: open-string licks, double-stop licks, scales, string bending, repetitive sequences, and chromatic licks. CD includes 99 demonstration tracks with each lick performed at two tempos.
00695599 Book/CDPack $16.95

COUNTRY CLASSICS FOR GUITAR • *arr. Fred Sokolow* **INCLUDES TAB**

30 favorites arranged for solo guitar, including: Always on My Mind • Blue Eyes Crying in the Rain • Crazy • Folsom Prison Blues • If You've Got the Money (I've Got the Time) • Make the World Go Away • Rocky Top • Walking the Floor over You • Your Cheatin' Heart • and more.
00699246 ....$14.95

FRETBOARD ROADMAPS – COUNTRY GUITAR **INCLUDES TAB**

The Essential Patterns That All the Pros Know and Use • *by Fred Sokolow*

This book/CD pack will teach you how to play lead and rhythm in the country style anywhere on the fretboard in any key. You'll play basic country progressions, boogie licks, steel licks, and other melodies and licks. You'll also learn a variety of lead guitar styles using moveable scale patterns, sliding scale patterns, chord-based licks, double-note licks, and more. The book features easy-to-follow diagrams and instructions for beginning, intermediate, and advanced players.
00695353 Book/CD Pack $12.95

SONGBOOK
COUNTRY GUITAR BIBLE

Note-for-note transcriptions with tab for 35 country classics, all in one hefty collection! Includes: Ain't Goin' Down ('Til the Sun Comes Up) • Big Time • Blue Eyes Crying in the Rain • Boot Scootin' Boogie • Cannon Ball Rag • Friends in Low Places • I'm So Lonesome I Could Cry • Little Sister • My Baby Thinks He's a Train • T-R-O-U-B-L-E • Wildwood Flower • and more.
00690465 Guitar Recorded Versions $19.95

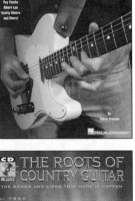

COUNTRY LICKS FOR GUITAR **INCLUDES TAB**

by Steve Trovato and Jerome Arnold

This unique package examines the lead guitar licks of the masters of country guitar, such as Chet Atkins, Jimmy Bryant, James Burton, Albert Lee, Scotty Moore, and many others! The accompanying CD includes demonstrations of each lick at normal and slow speeds. The instruction covers single-string licks, pedal-steel licks, open-string licks, chord licks, rockabilly licks, funky country licks, tips on fingerings, phrasing, technique, theory, and application.
00695577 Book/CD Pack............................$15.95

COUNTRY SOLOS FOR GUITAR **INCLUDES TAB**

by Steve Trovato

This unique book/CD pack lets guitarists examine the solo styles of axe masters such as Chet Atkins, James Burton, Ray Flacke, Albert Lee, Scotty Moore, Roy Nichols, Jerry Reed and others. It covers techniques including hot banjo rolls, funky double stops, pedal-steel licks, open-string licks and more, in standard notation and tab with phrase-by-phrase performance notes. The CD includes full demonstrations and rhythm-only tracks.
00695448 Book/CD Pack............................$17.95

THE ROOTS OF COUNTRY GUITAR **INCLUDES TAB**

The Songs and Licks That Made It Happen
by Fred Sokolow

A complete survey of a musical genre, its pioneers and how it developed, including: Six note-for-note transcriptions of famous tunes pivotal to the genre; extensive instruction in the essential playing styles that are to the genre, using scales, chords, licks, and musical exercises; the history of the development of each playing style; biographies of the pioneering artists; a recording of the songs, exercises, and licks. Songs include: Ballad of Thunder Road • Buckaroo • Cotton Fields (The Cotton Song) • Galloping on the Guitar • I Am a Pilgrim • Twin Guitar Special.
00699079 Book/CD Pack $14.95

RED-HOT COUNTRY GUITAR

by Michael Hawley

The complete guide to playing lead guitar in the styles of Pete Anderson, Danny Gatton, Albert Lee, Brent Mason, and more. Includes loads of red-hot licks, techniques, solos, theory and more.
00695831 Book/CD Pack $17.95

0308

HAL·LEONARD GUITAR PLAY·ALONG

This series will help you play your favorite songs quickly and easily. **INCLUDES TAB** Just follow the tab and listen to the CD to hear how the guitar should sound, and then play along using the separate backing tracks. Mac or PC users can also slow down the tempo without changing pitch by using the CD in their computer. The melody and lyrics are included in the book so that you can sing or simply follow along.

VOL. 1 – ROCK	00699570 / $16.99
VOL. 2 – ACOUSTIC	00699569 / $16.95
VOL. 3 – HARD ROCK	00699573 / $16.95
VOL. 4 – POP/ROCK	00699571 / $16.99
VOL. 5 – MODERN ROCK	00699574 / $16.99
VOL. 6 – '90s ROCK	00699572 / $16.99
VOL. 7 – BLUES	00699575 / $16.95
VOL. 8 – ROCK	00699585 / $14.95
VOL. 9 – PUNK ROCK	00699576 / $14.95
VOL. 10 – ACOUSTIC	00699586 / $16.95
VOL. 11 – EARLY ROCK	00699579 / $14.95
VOL. 12 – POP/ROCK	00699587 / $14.95
VOL. 13 – FOLK ROCK	00699581 / $14.95
VOL. 14 – BLUES ROCK	00699582 / $16.95
VOL. 15 – R&B	00699583 / $14.95
VOL. 16 – JAZZ	00699584 / $15.95
VOL. 17 – COUNTRY	00699588 / $15.95
VOL. 18 – ACOUSTIC ROCK	00699577 / $15.95
VOL. 19 – SOUL	00699578 / $14.95
VOL. 20 – ROCKABILLY	00699580 / $14.95
VOL. 21 – YULETIDE	00699602 / $14.95
VOL. 22 – CHRISTMAS	00699600 / $15.95
VOL. 23 – SURF	00699635 / $14.95
VOL. 24 – ERIC CLAPTON	00699649 / $16.95
VOL. 25 – LENNON & McCARTNEY	00699642 / $14.95
VOL. 26 – ELVIS PRESLEY	00699643 / $14.95
VOL. 27 – DAVID LEE ROTH	00699645 / $16.95
VOL. 28 – GREG KOCH	00699646 / $14.95
VOL. 29 – BOB SEGER	00699647 / $14.95
VOL. 30 – KISS	00699644 / $14.95
VOL. 31 – CHRISTMAS HITS	00699652 / $14.95
VOL. 32 – THE OFFSPRING	00699653 / $14.95
VOL. 33 – ACOUSTIC CLASSICS	00699656 / $16.95
VOL. 34 – CLASSIC ROCK	00699658 / $16.95
VOL. 35 – HAIR METAL	00699660 / $16.95
VOL. 36 – SOUTHERN ROCK	00699661 / $16.95
VOL. 37 – ACOUSTIC METAL	00699662 / $16.95
VOL. 38 – BLUES	00699663 / $16.95
VOL. 39 – '80s METAL	00699664 / $16.95
VOL. 40 – INCUBUS	00699668 / $16.95
VOL. 41 – ERIC CLAPTON	00699669 / $16.95
VOL. 42 – CHART HITS	00699670 / $16.95
VOL. 43 – LYNYRD SKYNYRD	00699681 / $17.95
VOL. 44 – JAZZ	00699689 / $14.95

VOL. 45 – TV THEMES	00699718 / $14.95
VOL. 46 – MAINSTREAM ROCK	00699722 / $16.95
VOL. 47 – HENDRIX SMASH HITS	00699723 / $17.95
VOL. 48 – AEROSMITH CLASSICS	00699724 / $14.95
VOL. 49 – STEVIE RAY VAUGHAN	00699725 / $16.95
VOL. 50 – NÜ METAL	00699726 / $14.95
VOL. 51 – ALTERNATIVE '90s	00699727 / $12.95
VOL. 52 – FUNK	00699728 / $14.95
VOL. 54 – HEAVY METAL	00699730 / $14.95
VOL. 55 – POP METAL	00699731 / $14.95
VOL. 56 – FOO FIGHTERS	00699749 / $14.95
VOL. 57 – SYSTEM OF A DOWN	00699751 / $14.95
VOL. 58 – BLINK-182	00699772 / $14.95
VOL. 59 – GODSMACK	00699773 / $14.95
VOL. 60 – 3 DOORS DOWN	00699774 / $14.95
VOL. 61 – SLIPKNOT	00699775 / $14.95
VOL. 62 – CHRISTMAS CAROLS	00699798 / $12.95
VOL. 63 – CREEDENCE CLEARWATER REVIVAL	00699802 / $16.99
VOL. 64 – THE ULTIMATE OZZY OSBOURNE	00699803 / $16.99
VOL. 65 – THE DOORS	00699806 / $16.99
VOL. 66 – THE ROLLING STONES	00699807 / $16.95
VOL. 67 – BLACK SABBATH	00699808 / $16.99
VOL. 68 – PINK FLOYD – DARK SIDE OF THE MOON	00699809 / $16.99
VOL. 69 – ACOUSTIC FAVORITES	00699810 / $14.95
VOL. 71 – CHRISTIAN ROCK	00699824 / $14.95
VOL. 72 – ACOUSTIC '90S	00699827 / $14.95
VOL. 74 – PAUL BALOCHE	00699831 / $14.95
VOL. 75 – TOM PETTY	00699882 / $16.99
VOL. 76 – COUNTRY HITS	00699884 / $14.95
VOL. 78 – NIRVANA	00700132 / $14.95
VOL. 80 – ACOUSTIC ANTHOLOGY	00700175 / $19.95
VOL. 81 – ROCK ANTHOLOGY	00700176 / $19.95
VOL. 82 – EASY SONGS	00700177 / $12.95
VOL. 83 – THREE CHORD SONGS	00700178 / $12.95
VOL. 96 – THIRD DAY	00700560 / $14.95
VOL. 97 – ROCK BAND	00700703 / $14.95
VOL. 98 – ROCK BAND	00700704 / $14.95

Prices, contents, and availability subject to change without notice.

FOR MORE INFORMATION, SEE YOUR LOCAL MUSIC DEALER,
OR WRITE TO:

HAL·LEONARD® CORPORATION

7777 W. BLUEMOUND RD. P.O. BOX 13819 MILWAUKEE, WI 53213

Visit Hal Leonard online at www.halleonard.com

Complete song lists available online.

GUITAR *signature licks*®

Signature Licks book/CD packs provide a step-by-step breakdown of "right from the record" riffs, licks, and solos so you can jam along with your favorite bands. They contain performance notes and an overview of each artist's or group's style, with note-for-note transcriptions in notes and tab. The CDs feature full-band demos at both normal and slow speeds.

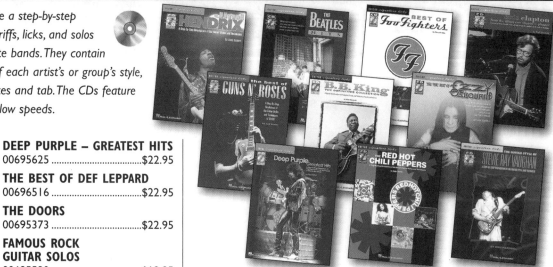

ACOUSTIC CLASSICS
00695864 ....$19.95

BEST OF ACOUSTIC GUITAR
00695640 ....$19.95

AEROSMITH 1973-1979
00695106 ....$22.95

AEROSMITH 1979-1998
00695219 ....$22.95

BEST OF AGGRO-METAL
00695592 ....$19.95

BEST OF CHET ATKINS
00695752 ....$22.95

THE BEACH BOYS DEFINITIVE COLLECTION
00695683 ....$22.95

BEST OF THE BEATLES FOR ACOUSTIC GUITAR
00695453 ....$22.95

THE BEATLES BASS
00695283 ....$22.95

THE BEATLES FAVORITES
00695096 ....$24.95

THE BEATLES HITS
00695049 ....$24.95

BEST OF GEORGE BENSON
00695418 ....$22.95

BEST OF BLACK SABBATH
00695249 ....$22.95

BEST OF BLINK - 182
00695704 ....$22.95

BEST OF BLUES GUITAR
00695846 ....$19.95

BLUES GUITAR CLASSICS
00695177 ....$19.95

BLUES/ROCK GUITAR MASTERS
00695348 ....$19.95

KENNY BURRELL
00695830 ....$22.95

BEST OF CHARLIE CHRISTIAN
00695584 ....$22.95

BEST OF ERIC CLAPTON
00695038 ....$24.95

ERIC CLAPTON – THE BLUESMAN
00695040 ....$22.95

ERIC CLAPTON – FROM THE ALBUM UNPLUGGED
00695250 ....$24.95

BEST OF CREAM
00695251 ....$22.95

CREEDANCE CLEARWATER REVIVAL
00695924 ....$22.95

DEEP PURPLE – GREATEST HITS
00695625 ....$22.95

THE BEST OF DEF LEPPARD
00696516 ....$22.95

THE DOORS
00695373 ....$22.95

FAMOUS ROCK GUITAR SOLOS
00695590 ....$19.95

BEST OF FOO FIGHTERS
00695481 ....$22.95

ROBBEN FORD
00695903 ....$22.95

GREATEST GUITAR SOLOS OF ALL TIME
00695301 ....$19.95

BEST OF GRANT GREEN
00695747 ....$22.95

GUITAR INSTRUMENTAL HITS
00695309 ....$19.95

GUITAR RIFFS OF THE '60S
00695218 ....$19.95

BEST OF GUNS N' ROSES
00695183 ....$22.95

HARD ROCK SOLOS
00695591 ....$19.95

JIMI HENDRIX
00696560 ....$24.95

HOT COUNTRY GUITAR
00695580 ....$19.95

BEST OF JAZZ GUITAR
00695586 ....$24.95

ERIC JOHNSON
00699317 ....$24.95

ROBERT JOHNSON
00695264 ....$22.95

THE ESSENTIAL ALBERT KING
00695713 ....$22.95

B.B. KING – THE DEFINITIVE COLLECTION
00695635 ....$22.95

THE KINKS
00695553 ....$22.95

BEST OF KISS
00699413 ....$22.95

MARK KNOPFLER
00695178 ....$22.95

LYNYRD SKYNYRD
00695872 ....$24.95

BEST OF YNGWIE MALMSTEEN
00695669 ....$22.95

BEST OF PAT MARTINO
00695632 ....$22.95

WES MONTGOMERY
00695387 ....$24.95

BEST OF NIRVANA
00695483 ....$24.95

THE OFFSPRING
00695852 ....$24.95

VERY BEST OF OZZY OSBOURNE
00695431 ....$22.95

BEST OF JOE PASS
00695730 ....$22.95

PINK FLOYD – EARLY CLASSICS
00695566 ....$22.95

THE POLICE
00695724 ....$22.95

THE GUITARS OF ELVIS
00696507 ....$22.95

BEST OF QUEEN
00695097 ....$24.95

BEST OF RAGE AGAINST THE MACHINE
00695480 ....$24.95

RED HOT CHILI PEPPERS
00695173 ....$22.95

RED HOT CHILI PEPPERS – GREATEST HITS
00695828 ....$24.95

BEST OF DJANGO REINHARDT
00695660 ....$24.95

BEST OF ROCK
00695884 ....$19.95

BEST OF ROCK 'N' ROLL GUITAR
00695559 ....$19.95

BEST OF ROCKABILLY GUITAR
00695785 ....$19.95

THE ROLLING STONES
00695079 ....$24.95

BEST OF JOE SATRIANI
00695216 ....$22.95

BEST OF SILVERCHAIR
00695488 ....$22.95

THE BEST OF SOUL GUITAR
00695703 ....$19.95

BEST OF SOUTHERN ROCK
00695560 ....$19.95

ROD STEWART
00695663 ....$22.95

BEST OF SURF GUITAR
00695822 ....$19.95

BEST OF SYSTEM OF A DOWN
00695788 ....$22.95

STEVE VAI
00673247 ....$22.95

STEVE VAI – ALIEN LOVE SECRETS: THE NAKED VAMPS
00695223 ....$22.95

STEVE VAI – FIRE GARDEN: THE NAKED VAMPS
00695166 ....$22.95

STEVE VAI – THE ULTRA ZONE: NAKED VAMPS
00695684 ....$22.95

STEVIE RAY VAUGHAN
00699316 ....$24.95

THE GUITAR STYLE OF STEVIE RAY VAUGHAN
00695155 ....$24.95

BEST OF THE VENTURES
00695772 ....$19.95

THE WHO
00695561 ....$22.95

BEST OF ZZ TOP
00695738 ....$24.95

Complete descriptions and songlists online!